NEW DIRECTIONS FOR STUDENT SERVICES

John H. Schuh, *Iowa State University*
EDITOR-IN-CHIEF

Elizabeth J. Whitt, *University of Iowa*
ASSOCIATE EDITOR

Creating Successful Partnerships Between Academic and Student Affairs

John H. Schuh
Iowa State University

Elizabeth J. Whitt
University of Iowa

EDITORS

Number 87, Fall 1999

JOSSEY-BASS PUBLISHERS
San Francisco

CREATING SUCCESSFUL PARTNERSHIPS BETWEEN ACADEMIC AND STUDENT
AFFAIRS
John H. Schuh, Elizabeth J. Whitt (eds.)
New Directions for Student Services, no. 87
John H. Schuh, Editor-in-Chief
Elizabeth J. Whitt, Associate Editor

Microfilm copies of issues and articles are available in 16mm and 35mm,
as well as microfiche in 105mm, through University Microfilms Inc., 300
North Zeeb Road, Ann Arbor, Michigan 48106-1346.

ISSN 0164-7970   ISBN 0-7879-4869-1

NEW DIRECTIONS FOR STUDENT SERVICES is part of The Jossey-Bass Higher
and Adult Education Series and is published quarterly by Jossey-Bass Inc.,
Publishers, 350 Sansome Street, San Francisco, California 94104-1342.
Periodicals postage paid at San Francisco, California, and at additional
mailing offices. Postmaster: Send address changes to New Directions for
Student Services, Jossey-Bass Inc., Publishers, 350 Sansome Street, San
Francisco, California 94104-1342.

New Directions for Student Services is indexed in College Student Personnel Abstracts and Contents Pages in Education.

SUBSCRIPTIONS cost $58.00 for individuals and $104.00 for institutions,
agencies, and libraries. See ordering information page at end of book.

EDITORIAL CORRESPONDENCE should be sent to the Editor-in-Chief,
John H. Schuh, N 243 Lagomarcino Hall, Iowa State University, Ames,
Iowa 50011

Cover photograph by Wernher Krutein/PHOTOVAULT © 1990.

Jossey-Bass Web address: www.josseybass.com

Manufactured in the United States of America on acid-free recycled paper
containing 100 percent recovered waste paper, of which at least 20 percent is postconsumer waste.

CONTENTS

EDITORS' NOTES

Collaboration is a common theme in the plethora of reports directed at improving higher education, particularly student outcomes. Reformers have called for increased collaboration and cooperation across academic disciplines (Boyer Commission on Educating Undergraduates in the Research University, 1998), between colleges and universities and the communities in which they live (Wingspread, 1993), and among students (National Association of State Universities and Land Grant Colleges, 1997). These calls are based on the assumption that optimum student learning cannot occur if the institutional components involved in that learning are separated from one another by structure or commitments or both (Kuh, 1996; Pascarella and Terenzini, 1991; Terenzini, Pascarella, and Blimling, 1996). In fact, "[Students] cannot be expected to connect the cognitive, intrapersonal, and interpersonal dimensions of their adult lives if their education has led them to believe these dimensions are unrelated. It is clear . . . that our current approach of bifurcating the cognitive and affective dimensions of learning does not work" (Baxter Magolda, 1996).

Few partnerships have received as much attention, however, as those between academic affairs, including faculty and administrators, and student affairs. Such partnerships are the *sine qua non* of "seamless learning environments" (American College Personnel Association, 1994; American College Personnel Association and National Association of Student Personnel Administrators, 1998; Kuh, 1996; Schroeder, 1999)—higher education environments that do not divide students' experiences with labels such as *academic* and *nonacademic* or *in-class* and *out-of-class* (Kuh, 1996; Kuh, Branch Douglas, Lund, and Ramin-Gyurnek, 1994; Kuh, Schuh, Whitt, and Associates, 1991). Rather, students are assisted to "use their life experiences to make meaning of material introduced in classes, laboratories, and studios, and to apply what they are learning in class to their lives outside the classroom" (Kuh, 1996, p. 136). *Seamless learning* thus implies a community of faculty and student affairs professionals working together to help students see their learning as taking place in all aspects of their college experiences.

Although partnerships between academic affairs and student affairs are widely recognized as important for student learning, as well as for institutional effectiveness, there is a great deal of evidence that such collaboration is more espoused than enacted (Kuh, 1997, 1998; Schroeder, 1999). Structural barriers limit communication, role demands limit common goals, time constraints limit opportunities for shared experiences, and insufficient communication limits recognition of shared commitments and interests. In the absence of specific goals or plans for developing partnerships, whatever good intentions there might be to foster seamless learning can languish unfulfilled.

This sourcebook is intended to help student affairs and academic affairs professionals identify strategies for collaboration by describing and analyzing actual academic and student affairs partnerships at a variety of types of institutions.

In Chapter One, Charles C. Schroeder provides a foundation for the rest of the sourcebook by exploring the reasons for establishing partnerships between academic and student affairs. The questions, "Why collaboration?" and "Why now?" are addressed.

Chapters Two through Five offer case studies and examples of collaborative partnerships at a variety of institutions. Barbara Jacoby begins the series with a description of how service-learning has served as a vehicle for faculty affairs and student affairs partnerships.

Freshman Interest Groups, commonly known as FIGs, demonstrate the need for, and influence of, collaboration between student affairs and academic affairs in creating seamless learning environments. In Chapter Three, Charles C. Schroeder, Frankie D. Minor, and Theodore A. Tarkow provide a detailed description of the development and implementation of the FIGs program at the University of Missouri-Columbia. In Chapter Four, Sarah B. Westfall's discussion of the many opportunities for collaboration at Indiana University also highlights FIGs.

In Chapter Five, Martin F. Larréy and Sandra M. Estanek offer a case study focused on partnerships at a small private college. The authors explore the impetus for the Ursuline Studies Program at Ursuline College (Ohio), and describe the collaborative efforts that led to the success of that program.

Some institutions have created partnerships by merging academic and student affairs into a single organizational unit. In Chapter Six, Jerry Price describes the strengths and limitations of such mergers, and discusses critical issues to consider in making a merger effective, particularly for students.

The sourcebook concludes with a look at evaluation by revisiting the key points of the preceding chapters. Building on the work of the other authors, John H. Schuh provides a set of principles to use in determining the effectiveness of partnerships and the climate for collaboration at individual institutions.

Elizabeth J. Whitt
John H. Schuh
Editors

References

American College Personnel Association. *The Student Learning Imperative: Implications for Student Affairs.* Alexandria, Va.: American College Personnel Association, 1994.

American College Personnel Association and National Association of Student Personnel Administrators. *Principles of Good Practice for Student Affairs.* Washington, D.C.: American College Personnel Association and National Association of Student Personnel Administrators, 1998.

Baxter Magolda, M. B. "Cognitive Learning and Personal Development: A False Dichotomy." *About Campus, 1* (3), 16–21.

Boyer Commission on Educating Undergraduates in the Research University. *Reinventing Undergraduate Education: A Blueprint for America's Research Universities*. New York: Carnegie Foundation for the Advancement of Teaching, 1998.

Kuh, G. D. "Guiding Principles for Creating Seamless Learning Environments for Undergraduates." *Journal of College Student Development*, 1996, *37*, 135–148.

Kuh, G. D. "You Gotta Believe!" *About Campus*, 1997, *2* (4), 2–3.

Kuh, G. D. "Lessons from the Mountains." *About Campus*, 1998, *3* (2), 16–21.

Kuh, G. D., Branch Douglas, K., Lund, J. P., Ramin-Gyurnick, J. *Student Learning Outside the Classroom: Transcending Artificial Boundaries*. Washington, D.C.: George Washington University, 1994. (ASHE-ERIC Higher Education Report no. 8.)

Kuh, G. D., Schuh, J. H., Whitt, E. J., and Associates. *Involving Colleges: Successful Approaches to Fostering Student Learning and Personal Development Outside the Classroom*. San Francisco: Jossey-Bass, 1991.

National Association of State Universities and Land Grant Colleges. *Returning to Our Roots: The Student Experience*. Washington, D.C.: National Association of State Universities and Land Grant Colleges, 1997.

Pascarella, E., and Terenzini, P. *How College Affects Students*. San Francisco: Jossey-Bass, 1991.

Schroeder, C. C. "Forging Educational Partnerships to Advance Student Learning." In G. S. Blimling and E. J. Whitt (eds.), *Good Practice in Student Affairs: Principles to Foster Student Learning*. San Francisco: Jossey-Bass, 1999.

Terenzini, P. T., Pascarella, E. T., Blimling, G. S. "Students' Out-of-Class Experiences and Their Influence on Learning and Cognitive Development: A Literature Review." *Journal of College Student Development*, 1996, *37*, 149–162.

Wingspread Group on Higher Education. *An American Imperative: Higher Expectations for Higher Education*. Racine, Wisc.: Johnson Foundation, 1993.

JOHN H. SCHUH is professor of higher education at Iowa State University.

ELIZABETH J. WHITT is associate professor in student development in postsecondary education at the University of Iowa.

Partnerships between academic and student affairs advance student learning, foster educational attainment, and reinvigorate undergraduate education.

Partnerships: An Imperative for Enhancing Student Learning and Institutional Effectiveness

Charles C. Schroeder

Few would dispute that the landscape of higher education is being altered dramatically. Faced with enormous, almost overwhelming, internal and external challenges, colleges and universities are seeking ways to improve undergraduate education by connecting undergraduate experiences with student learning. To accomplish these objectives, "student affairs professionals attempt to make seamless what are often perceived by students to be disjointed, unconnected experiences by bridging organizational boundaries and forging collaborative partnerships with faculty and others to enhance student learning" (American College Personnel Association [ACPA], 1994, p. 3).

This chapter explores the importance of forging partnerships between academic affairs and student affairs—partnerships that advance student learning, foster educational attainment, and reinvigorate undergraduate education. The first section builds the case for partnerships by addressing two questions: (1) Why partnerships?, and (2) Why now? Descriptions of the nature of partnerships, their benefits, and obstacles to their formation follow. The chapter concludes with a discussion of implications for the future of academic and student affairs partnerships.

Why Partnerships? Why Now?

In the introduction to the widely heralded report, *An American Imperative: Higher Expectations for Higher Education* (1993), the Wingspread Group concluded: "A disturbing and dangerous mismatch exists between what American society needs of higher education and what it is receiving. Nowhere is the mismatch more dangerous than in the quality of undergraduate preparation provided on many campuses. The American imperative for the twenty-first century is that society must hold higher education to much higher expectations or risk a national decline" (p. 1). The call for reform of undergraduate education comes not only from documents such as *An American Imperative* and the recent Kellogg Commission reports issued on behalf of the National Association of State Universities and Land Grant Colleges (National Association of State Universities and Land Grant Colleges [NASULGC], 1997), but also from the popular press, such as *Newsweek, USA Today,* and *The New York Times.* These reports persistently question the rapid rise in college costs; low retention and graduation rates; the primacy of research over teaching; inefficiency, duplication, and waste; greater gaps between ideal academic standards and actual student performance; lack of service and institutional assistance to local communities and states; and deteriorating public trust in the higher education enterprise. Legislators, state coordinating boards, and other powerful external constituents increasingly demand greater emphasis on access, affordability, and accountability—particularly enhanced performance and productivity—while, in many instances, simultaneously reducing funding levels (Levine, 1997).

To address the preceding challenges, many institutions have begun to focus more attention on reinvigorating undergraduate education by fostering collaboration and cross-functional dialogue between personnel in student affairs and academic affairs. These institutions are beginning to respond to the challenge posed by Terenzini and Pascarella (1994): "Organizationally and operationally, we have lost sight of the forest. If undergraduate education is to be enhanced, faculty members, joined by academic and student affairs administrators, must devise ways to deliver undergraduate education that are as comprehensive and integrated as the ways that students actually learn. A whole new mindset is needed to capitalize on the interrelatedness of the in- and out-of-class influences on student learning and the functional interconnectedness of academic and student affairs divisions" (p. 32).

Terenzini and Pascarella appear to be arguing for the creation of "seamless learning environments"—settings where in-class and out-of-class experiences are mutually supporting and where institutional resources are marshaled and channeled to achieve complementary learning outcomes (Kuh, 1996, 1997). Learning environments such as these bind together in a whole and continuous fashion what once was believed to be separate, distinct parts to achieve the "seamless coat of learning" proposed some seventy years ago by Alfred North Whitehead (1929).

Because seamless learning environments comprise a network of interdependent components that work together to accomplish a common end, they can address the age-old "part-whole problem"—the lack of coherence in undergraduate learning experiences (Plater, 1998). Contrast the ideals of coherence and integration with the current reality of many student experiences. Students' academic experiences are often subdivided into discrete and disjointed general education courses and courses in the major. Cocurricular experiences are disconnected from academic experiences. Classroom facilities are geographically isolated from residence halls. Campus employment opportunities have no relationship with academic or cocurricular goals, and academic advising and career planning are like two ships passing in the night. And the goals and outcomes of general education are rarely, if ever, addressed as a core experience in new student orientation (Schroeder, 1999). In view of realities such as these, where do students, faculty, and student affairs educators find the connections, the integration, and the coherence that is the essence of holistic education?

Ironically, institutions that constitute one of the greatest threats to traditional institutions of higher education—new providers such as the University of Phoenix and the Western Governors' University (Marchese, 1998)—are becoming exemplars of seamless learning. These institutions look at the whole student rather than only at the student in the classroom. According to Plater (1998), they "connect each course to other courses—and to important student services such as career counseling—and they link all courses together into meaningful, cumulative, accessible, and certifiable wholes—like the lives of students" (p. 12). In 1998, the Boyer Commission report, *Reinventing Undergraduate Education: A Blueprint for America's Research Universities*, strongly endorsed a model of undergraduate education similar to the one promoted by the new providers—a model that "makes the baccalaureate experience an inseparable part of an integrated whole" (p. 7).

Because seamless learning environments are integrated systems, their design and maintenance require high levels of collaboration so that organizational arrangements and processes can be linked and aligned appropriately (Bloland, Stamatakos, and Rogers, 1996). Partnerships between academic affairs and student affairs are the primary venues for creating and sustaining educational settings such as these.

The Nature of Partnerships

On the surface, a definition of partners or partnership appears relatively simple—"associate or colleague; one of two or more who work or play together" (Webster, 1996, p. 859). A second definition from the same source, however, is more interesting and compelling: "One of the heavy timbers that strengthens a ship's deck to support a mast" (p. 859). The latter meaning provides a powerful metaphor for the support that partners provide each other in meeting the demands of their work. Ideally, partners have a strong relationship; they are comfortable working together and have an appreciation one for the other. Communication in effective partnerships is excellent, and relationships are open and honest. These partners trust each other, and differences of opinion are negotiated within the context of respect, comfort, and honesty.

The process of developing an effective partnership, whether between or among people or between units in student affairs and academic affairs, is complex and takes time, energy, and commitment. Potential partners who value the idea of partnership and the likely benefits of partnership must commit themselves to the systematic development of the partnership. In this regard, the notion of sharing is of great importance in developing and sustaining effective partnerships. Partners share work, planning, goal setting, decision making, and problem solving, as well as vision, philosophy, values, and ideas. Other attributes associated with successful partnerships include cooperation, assertiveness, responsibility, communication, autonomy, and coordination (Norsen, Opladen, and Quinn, 1995).

In addition to the attributes previously mentioned, the following principles can be very useful in guiding the development of partnerships between academic and student affairs (Schroeder, Minor, and Tarkow, 1999):

Partnerships are successful when they are developed from a common reference point or common purpose—a shared vision of undergraduate education, an institutional problem (that is, poor retention and graduation rates), or a major triggering event (that is, externally imposed undergraduate education mandate).

Successful partnerships involve cross-functional teams, joint planning and implementation, and assessment of mutually agreed upon outcomes.

Effective partnerships require thinking and acting systemically by linking and aligning a variety of resources—human, fiscal, and so on—to achieve desired results.

Partnerships require senior administrators in academic and student affairs to be strong champions and advocates for innovation and change and they must make visible their commitments to developing, nurturing, and sustaining partnerships.

Effective partnerships occasionally require participants to step out of their comfort zones, challenge prevailing assumptions, and take reasonable risks.

Obstacles and Constraints to Forging Partnerships

Although the development of partnerships has been an espoused value for student affairs educators for decades, a variety of obstacles and constraints have made forging effective partnerships between academic affairs and student affairs difficult to achieve.

In an insightful and compelling essay, *Classroom and Context: An Educational Dialectic,* Blake (1979) describes one of the principal obstacles to collaboration between student affairs and academic affairs: "People in student affairs, knowing that education is, after all, the mission of their institution, justify their activities as educational. Yet the more they do this, the less often they convince their faculty colleagues. A persistent gap seems to exist between the two groups of people on campus who work most closely with students" (p. 280).

This persistent gap is evident in the historical separation of the formal curriculum from the informal cocurriculum as well as the prevailing view that the role of student affairs is ancillary, supplementary, or complementary to the academic mission of the institution. As Young (1996) indicates, these concerns are not new, but rather deeply embedded issues that carry long histories within student affairs and higher education. Young attributes this gap to fundamental differences between two dominant orientations—an organic perspective and a functional perspective. The organic perspective, best exemplified by the 1937 *Student Personnel Point of View* (National Association of Student Personnel Administrators [NASPA], 1989), advanced a philosophy of education that focused on educating the whole student and reminded everyone on campus, especially faculty, of their role in achieving this institutional objective. Yet although the *Student Personnel Point of View* preaches integration, the practice of student affairs, particularly during the past thirty years, reflects specialization and segregation. As a result, most student affairs divisions have become isolated and even estranged from the academic mission of their institutions (Bloland, Stamatakos, and Rogers, 1996).

Isolation and fragmentation have resulted from the exponential growth of higher education during the past fifty years. In response to burgeoning enrollments, rapid expansion of knowledge, proliferation of disciplines, and increasingly diverse student populations, institutions have attempted to address increased complexity through creating highly specialized hierarchical organizations. Specialization, in turn, has led to compartmentalization and fragmentation, often resulting in what is popularly described as *functional silos* or *mine shafts*. These vertical structures, though often effective at promoting interaction within functional units, often create obstacles to interaction, coordination, and collaboration between and among units. According to Bonser (1992), "not only are there barriers between disciplines, departments, and schools, too often warring factions exist within the units themselves" (p. 511). Developing a shared vision and collective responsibility for that vision is very difficult when fragmentation and compartmentalization foster insularity.

Faculty, in particular, may view their department as the last bulwark against a hostile and confusing environment in which outsiders (student affairs administrators, politicians, and so on) may make unreasonable demands and even threaten academic freedom (Lovett, 1994). As a result, many campuses— especially large public universities—are characterized not by a sense of community, but rather by a constellation of independent principalities and fiefdoms, each disconnected from the others and from any common institutional purpose or transcending values.

Tightly coupled bureaucratic organizations, with their emphasis on control and stability rather than on innovation, encourage a sense of predictability, which in turn provides a sense of dominance, security, and control—conditions essential for organizational identity and esteem (Schroeder, Nicholls, and Kuh, 1983; Seymour, 1995). Many divisions and departments strive for stability and predictability by creating systems to maintain balance and continuity. There is often great reluctance to changing established practices that may have worked well, whether or not they are working well currently. Familiar phrases such as, "We've never done it that way before," and, "We tried it, but it didn't work," are all too common. Forging effective partnerships to advance learning, however, requires overcoming this tyranny of custom. Seymour (1995) alludes to the potentially paralyzing influence of routine and conventional practices when he states, "Most organizations have shared assumptions that protect the status quo and provide few opportunities for learning. Standard operating procedures can become so institutionalized that competence becomes associated with how well one adheres to the rules" (p. 101).

Forging educational partnerships also requires assertive, effective leadership—leadership that challenges prevailing assumptions and encourages reasonable risk taking. As Senge (1990) suggests, a primary role of leaders is to "bring to the surface and challenge prevailing mental models" (p. 9). Major obstacles to forging partnerships include fundamental differences in core assumptions and mental models exhibited by campus constituencies. For example, faculty, student affairs professionals, academic administrators, and students often have widely differing views regarding the relative merits of in-class and out-of-class activities (Kuh, Douglas, Lund, and Ramin-Gyurnek, 1994; Whitt, 1996).

Well-intentioned efforts to create partnerships often are derailed because of competing assumptions about what constitutes learning and effective undergraduate education (Kuh, 1997). The primacy of the curriculum and course work (particularly in the major) are highly valued by faculty whereas informal learning that occurs through out-of-class experiences is not. On many campuses undergraduate education is narrowly defined by faculty as general education or core curriculum requirements—no reference is made to the value or impact of out-of-class experiences on desired undergraduate education outcomes (such as critical thinking, communications skills, humanitarian values, and so on).

Faculty also focus their efforts on facilitating the cognitive and intellectual development of students, whereas student affairs educators promote affective, psychosocial dimensions of students' personal development (Terenzini and Pascarella, 1994). In addition, institutional rewards for faculty are based on research productivity, scholarship, and teaching rather than on collaborative initiatives with student affairs. Diverging views, assumptions, and rewards such as these are rooted in different institutional cultures and these cultures must be understood and appreciated if partnerships are to be developed and sustained (Kuh and Whitt, 1988).

Blake (1979, 1996) has suggested some additional cultural differences between faculty and student affairs educators in terms of their personality styles, educational preparation, values, and purposes that can contribute to a communication gap. Faculty often value independent creation and dissemination of knowledge, whereas student affairs educators value holistic student development and collaboration. Faculty prize thinking, reflection, and collegiality (self-governance and a flat hierarchy) over doing, whereas student affairs values teamwork (acceptance of structure and differentiated hierarchy) and doing over thinking and reflecting (Love, Jacobs, Poschini, Hardy, and Kuh,

1993). Furthermore, faculty disciplinary differences, such as differences between pure and applied fields and "hard" and "soft" disciplines, affect not only the way faculty approach their work but also have a direct impact on student affairs and faculty collaborations (Eimers, forthcoming). Simply having different values, assumptions, and responsibilities does not mean that student affairs professionals and faculty members cannot work together or that conflict is inevitable. To the contrary, if properly acknowledged and utilized, these differences can, at times, enrich and strengthen partnerships (Blake, 1996).

Potential Learning Outcomes and Conditions that Promote Them

In the recent report, *Returning to Our Roots: The Student Experience* (NASULGC, 1997), the authors state: "The biggest educational challenge we face revolves around developing character, conscience, citizenship, tolerance, civility, and individual and social responsibility in our students. We dare not ignore this obligation in a society that sometimes gives the impression that virtues such as these are discretionary. These should be part of the standard equipment of our graduates, not options" (p. 13).

Concern for the cultivation of these virtues is certainly not a new imperative for higher education; in fact, stressing the education of the "whole person" has been a primary purpose of higher learning throughout the ages. Indeed, it was the focal point of a seminal essay, *The Idea of a University*, written by John Henry Newman in 1852 while he served as a tutor at Oriel College of Oxford University. His essay reminds us that liberal learning "is the great ordinary means to a great but ordinary end," and that "its end is fitness for the world" (Davis and Schroeder, 1982, p.155). The current challenge, however, is to translate Newman's words into educational goals and outcomes and to forge partnerships that foster their attainment.

Because partnerships between academic affairs and student affairs should be based on a shared vision of undergraduate education, it is essential to define potential learning outcomes that should result from their implementation. Kuh (1993) delineates a number of learning outcome clusters, all of which are eloquently expressed in Newman's *Idea of a University* (Newman, 1979), recent reform reports on undergraduate education, and the *Student Learning Imperative* (ACPA, 1994):

Cognitive complexity—Reflective thought, critical thinking, quantitative reasoning, and intellectual flexibility.
Knowledge acquisition and application—Understanding knowledge from a range of disciplines and the ability to relate knowledge to daily life.
Humanitarianism—An understanding and appreciation of human differences.
Inter-personal and intra-personal competence—A coherent, integrative constellation of personal attributes such as identity, self-esteem, confidence, integrity, and sense of civic responsibility.

Practical competence—Skills reflected in enhancing the capacity to manage one's personal affairs, to be economically self-sufficient and vocationally competent.

These learning outcomes, and the approaches and conditions that facilitate their attainment, are essential perspectives and tools for addressing a variety of issues and opportunities in undergraduate education through collaborative partnerships. Faculty and academic administrators, however, tend to focus their efforts on the first two outcome clusters—cognitive complexity and knowledge acquisition and application—whereas student affairs educators have embraced the remaining ones. This practice of separating undergraduate experiences into distinct, disconnected components fails to capitalize on what we have learned from over fifty years of research on college impact—that cognitive and affective development are inextricably intertwined and that the curriculum and out-of-class activities are not discrete, independent variables, but rather affect each other in profound ways (Pascarella and Terenzini, 1991). Hence, what is needed is a new integrated view of the learning process: "When learning and personal development are integrated, the cognitive and affective dimensions are seen as one process, and the hallmark of a successful educational experience is when increased cognitive understanding is complemented by increased sense of self, personal maturity, and interpersonal effectiveness" (King and Baxter Magolda, 1996, p. 163).

Decades of research in educational psychology, instructional design, and, more recently, cognitive science reveal a number of approaches and conditions that promote integrated learning and facilitate the achievement of various learning outcomes. Chief among these are approaches that emphasize application and experience, link established concepts to new situations, emphasize interpersonal collaborations, consistently promote clearly identified cross-disciplinary skills that are publicly held to be important, and emphasize rich and frequent feedback on performance (Ewell, 1997). Additional conditions have been enumerated in *Seven Principles of Good Practice in Undergraduate Education* (Johnson Foundation, 1987) and in *Principles of Good Practice for Student Affairs* (American College Personnel Association and National Association of Student Personnel Administrators, 1998) and *Making Quality Count* (Education Commission of the States, 1995).

A number of strategic indicators often result from effective educational partnerships between academic affairs and student affairs. These include improved student satisfaction, academic achievement, persistence, and graduation rates and gains in general education outcomes. Effective partnerships also enhance students' cognitive and psychosocial development and foster their academic and social integration. Other indicators often associated with successful partnerships include students' higher levels of integration of course information, increased student-faculty interaction, and, perhaps most important, substantially higher levels of overall student learning.

Institutional Issues, Opportunities, and Benefits

Partnerships that respond to pressing institutional issues can be quite successful in reinvigorating undergraduate education (Schroeder, 1999). Although critical issues differ between and among institutions, the following opportunities often lend themselves to a collaborative response on the part of individuals in academic and student affairs:

1. Improving retention and graduation rates by enhancing student success; increasing success rates in high-risk courses, particularly for first- and second-year students
2. Creating active learning opportunities that respond to the learning styles of new students
3. Enhancing multicultural awareness, understanding, and respect; fostering civic engagement and leadership through service learning; establishing and articulating institutional expectations
4. Extending the definition of general education outcomes to include knowledge and skills gained through cocurricular experiences; fostering higher levels of educational attainment for students in historically underrepresented groups
5. Improving the effectiveness of advising
6. Humanizing large lecture classes through implementing innovative pedagogy that encourages more time on task
7. Enhancing students' writing performance
8. Developing learning communities that enhance faculty and student interaction and provide integration and coherence among various disciplines and cocurricular experiences
9. Increasing the utilization of technology to enhance teaching and learning
10. Reconciling diversity and community
11. Expanding institutional assessment initiatives to include learning outcomes that reflect more than content mastery—outcomes such as humanitarian values, character development, communication skills, and inter- and intrapersonal competence.

These issues are, of course, not discrete (Pascarella and Terenzini, 1991). For example, increasing success rates in high-risk courses generally improves retention and graduation rates. Enhancing multicultural awareness and understanding strengthens campus community and fosters higher levels of educational attainment for students of color. Learning communities not only provide integration and coherence among various disciplines and cocurricular experiences, they also enhance academic achievement, social and academic integration, and retention. To be sure, creating seamless learning environments through collaborative partnerships address the interdependent nature of these institutional issues. Although future chapters in this sourcebook highlight some of these partnerships, the following suggestions illustrate approaches worth considering.

On many campuses, faculty continue to be bewildered and frustrated with the students they see in their classrooms today. Unfamiliar with many of the new characteristics, faculty see contemporary students as hopelessly under-prepared, or less bright or motivated than previous generations. These new students (Schroeder, 1993) view knowledge and derive meaning in vastly dif-ferent ways than those of their instructors. Their learning styles are character-ized by a preference for direct, concrete experiences; moderate to high degrees of structure; linear, sequential learning; and often a need to know why before doing something. In general, these students' learning patterns prefer the con-crete, the practical, and the immediate—characteristics that are opposite, and often antagonistic, to those of faculty. Creating a better match between new student learning styles and instructional approaches would be an admirable goal for a partnership between academic affairs and student affairs.

Because new student learning patterns respond to active modes of teach-ing and learning, partnerships that connect, in a seamless fashion, formal cur-ricular experiences with informal cocurricular experiences can be particularly effective in promoting student success. For example, student affairs staff can develop partnerships with staff in the campus writing program and faculty who teach freshmen composition courses. Since the primary purpose of these courses is to develop students' writing skills, the content of the courses often varies considerably. Student affairs staff, in partnership with faculty members, can design a range of active learning experiences—such as case method approaches, service learning, or field experiences—that connect students with writing assignments. Important campus issues such as multiculturalism, binge drinking, or male-female relationships could be the focal point of writing assignments. Similar partnerships could be developed with faculty who teach philosophy and ethics courses. In these instances, student affairs staff could develop videotaped vignettes of students discussing moral dilemmas in their residence halls as well as their fraternity and sorority houses. The videos could be catalysts for class discussions of various philosophical and ethical perspec-tives on resolving dilemmas such as those illustrated in the vignettes.

Finally, when student affairs staff work with faculty to develop effective cocurricular experiences such as field trips, the level of student engagement in the content of courses increases exponentially. For example, on one campus a Freshman Interest Group (FIG) with twenty students, coenrolled in three courses built around the theme of "variety of human experience," traveled with their instructors to Native-American burial mounds in Illinois. The religious studies professor discussed the religious significance of the mounds, the anthropology professor pointed out the cultural and archeological meaning, and the writing instructor asked the students to integrate their class readings and field experiences into a writing assignment (Schroeder, Minor, and Tarkow, 1999). By actively engaging students in the subject matter through an effective field experience, the instructors and the student affairs cofacilitator were able to bring a degree of integration and coherence among the various disciplines of the FIG.

Student affairs professionals also can form partnerships with staff in the learning center and faculty in the math department to improve performance in high-risk courses such as college algebra and calculus. Programs such as math TV can be offered over the residence hall movie network, and supplemental instruction and subject mastery workshops can be provided in residential units. Civic leadership residential colleges can be designed by cross-functional teams including residential life staff, faculty from political science, staff from the center for service learning, and officers from various ROTC programs. Staff in student life and the career center also can develop partnerships with academic administrators and department chairs to create multimedia, interactive software programs that help students assess their skills and competencies and identify out-of-class experiences that are designed to strengthen them. Electronic portfolios such as these can also be useful in improving the effectiveness of advising and educational planning by serving as decision-support systems for students with different academic interests and aspirations. Finally, partnerships could be forged between staff in orientation, corporate recruiters, and faculty responsible for general education to ensure that general education goals, objectives, and outcomes are a major foci of summer orientation programs and freshmen success courses.

Partnerships that create interventions such as these are successful because they create integrated, seamless learning experiences by linking and aligning resources in a cross-functional fashion. Additional examples of effective partnerships are described in the 1998 report *Powerful Partnerships: A Shared Responsibility for Learning,* issued by American Association for Higher Education (AAHE), American College Personnel Association (ACPA), and National Association of Student Personnel Administrators (NASPA).

Appropriate responses to institutional issues and opportunities such as these will vary depending upon the mission, purpose, and size of the institution. On relatively small campuses, partnerships often focus interventions at the institutional level, whereas on larger campuses, the importance of these issues usually varies by setting (college, school, department, or other units); therefore, partnerships should be developed to address them at the microlevel (Schroeder and Hurst, 1996). Two primary strategies for identifying issues such as these are boundary spanning and environmental assessment—both of which require individuals to venture beyond the comfort, predictability, and security provided by their organizational boundaries to identify the opportunities and their relative value to key stakeholders.

Implications for the Future

Colleges and universities across the country attempt to reform undergraduate education by improving student learning productivity, increasing success rates, enhancing multicultural understanding, and achieving higher levels of educational attainment. The critical challenge faced by most of these institutions is to make student experiences educationally purposeful by marshalling and aligning resources through effective partnerships to create seamless learning environments. Addressing this challenge requires new forms of educational and administrative leadership: "Our challenges are no longer technical issues of how to allocate rising revenues, but difficult adaptive problems of how to lead when conditions are constantly changing, resources are tight, expectations are high, and options are limited. We live in an age of transformational, not technical, change. Our leadership, like our institutions, must become transformational as well" (NASULGC, 1997, p. v).

In his book, *The Courage to Teach,* Parker Palmer (1998) describes the nature of transformational leadership by sharing a story about Rosa Parks, who on December 1, 1955, in Montgomery, Alabama, decided to live her life divided no more. She did a very simple, yet heroic thing—she sat down in the whites-only front section of a segregated bus and refused to yield her seat to a white man. This courageous act was the catalyst that launched the civil rights movement—a movement that eventually transformed American society.

Colleges and universities can also be transformed if they are willing to create new, collaborative campus cultures (Rice, 1998). These are cultures in which "people continually expand their capacity to create the results they truly desire, where new and expansive patterns of thinking are nurtured, where collective aspiration is set free, and where people are continually learning how to learn together" (Senge, 1990, p. 1).

If colleges and universities are to address successfully the multitude of internal and external challenges they currently face, personnel in academic affairs and student affairs must choose, as Rosa Parks chose, to live divided no more. They must embrace an integrated view of learning and forge effective educational partnerships that advance student learning, foster educational attainment, and reinvigorate undergraduate education. To do less would diminish the potential of our institutions, ourselves, and most important, our students.

References

American Association for Higher Education, American College Personnel Association, and National Association of Student Personnel Administrators. *Powerful Partnerships: A Shared Responsibility for Learning.* Washington, D.C.: American Association for Higher Education, American College Personnel Association, National Association of Student Personnel Administrators, 1998.

American College Personnel Association. *The Student Learning Imperative: Implications for Student Affairs.* Washington, D.C.: American College Personnel Association, 1994.

American College Personnel Association and National Association of Student Personnel Administrators. *Principles of Good Practice for Student Affairs.* Washington, D.C.: American College Personnel Association and National Association of Student Personnel Administrators, 1998.

Blake, E. S. "Classroom and Context: An Educational Dialectic." *Academe,* 1979, *65,* 280–292.

Blake, E. S. "The Yin and Yang of Student Learning in College." *About Campus,* 1996, *1* (4), 4–9.

Bloland, P. A., Stamatakos, L. C., and Rogers, R. R. "Redirecting the Role of Student Affairs to Focus on Student Learning." *Journal of College Student Development,* 1996, *37* (2), 217–226.

Bonser, C. F. "Total Quality Education." *Public Administration Review,* 1992, *52* (5), 504–512.

Boyer Commission on Educating Undergraduates in the Research University. *Reinventing Undergraduate Education: A Blueprint for America's Research Universities.* New York: The Carnegie Foundation for the Advancement of Teaching, 1998.

Davis, M., and Schroeder, C. C. "New Students in Liberal Arts Colleges: Threat or Challenge?" In N. J. Watson and L. R. Stevens (eds.), *Pioneers and Pallbearers: Perspectives on Liberal Education.* Macon, Ga.: Mercer University Press, 1982, 147–168.

Education Commission of the States. *Making Quality Count.* Denver: Education Commission of the States, 1995.

Eimers, M. T. "The Discipline Affiliation of Faculty: Understanding the Differences and the Implications for Student Affairs and Faculty Collaboration." *About Campus,* forthcoming.

Ewell, P. T. "Organizing for Learning: A New Imperative." *AAHE Bulletin,* 1997, *49* (5), 3–6.

Johnson Foundation. *Seven Principles of Good Practice in Undergraduate Education.* Racine, Wisc.: Johnson Foundation, 1987.

King, P. M., and Baxter Magolda, M.B.D. "A Developmental Perspective on Learning." *Journal of College Student Development,* 1996, *37* (2), 163–173.

Kuh, G. D. "In Their Words: What Students Learn Outside the Classroom." *American Educational Research Journal,* 1993, *30* (2), 277–304.

Kuh, G. D., "Guiding Principles for Creating Seamless Learning Environments for Undergraduates." *Journal of College Student Development,* 1996, *37* (2), 135–148.

Kuh, G. D., "Working Together to Enhance Student Learning Inside and Outside the Classroom." Paper presented at the annual AAHE Assessment and Quality Conference, Miami, Florida, June 1997.

Kuh, G. D., Douglas, K. D., Lund, J. P., and Ramin-Gyurnek, J. *Student Learning Outside the Classroom: Transcending Artificial Boundaries.* Washington, D.C.: The George Washington University, 1994. (ASHE/ERIC Higher Education Report, No. 8.)

Kuh, G. D., and Whitt, E. J. *The Invisible Tapestry: Culture in American Colleges and Universities.* Washington, D.C.: The George Washington University, 1988. (ASHE/ERIC Higher Education Report, No. 1.)

Levine, A., "Higher Education Becomes a Mature Industry." *About Campus,* 1997, *2* (3), 31–32.

Love, P. G., Jacobs, B. A., Poschini, V. J., Hardy, C. M., and Kuh, G. D. "Student Culture." In G. D. Kuh (ed.), *Cultural Perspectives in Student Affairs Work.* Washington, D.C.: American College Personnel Association, 1993.

Lovett, C. "Assessment, CQI, and Faculty Culture." In *CQI 101: A First Reader for Higher Education.* Washington, D. C.: American Association for Higher Education, 1994.

Marchese, T. "Not-So-Distant Competitors: How New Providers Are Remaking the Post-Secondary Marketplace." *AAHE Bulletin,* 1998, *50* (9), 3–7.

National Association of State Universities and Land Grant Colleges. *Returning to Our Roots: The Student Experience.* Washington, D.C.: National Association of State Universities and Land Grant Colleges, 1997.

National Association of Student Personnel Administrators. *Points of View.* Washington, D.C.: National Association of Student Personnel Administrators, 1989.

Newman, J. H. "The Idea of a University." In M. H. Abrams (ed.), *The Norton Anthology of English Literature.* New York: Norton, 1979.

Norsen, L., Opladen, J., and Quinn, J. "Practice Model: Collaborative Practice." *Critical Care Nursing Clinics of North America,* 1995, *7* (1), 43–52.

Palmer, P. J. *The Courage to Teach.* San Francisco: Jossey-Bass, 1998.

Pascarella, E. T., and Terenzini, P. T. *How College Affects Students: Findings and Insights from 20 Years of Research.* San Francisco: Jossey-Bass, 1991.

Plater, W. M. "So Why Aren't We Taking Learning Seriously?" *About Campus*, 1998, 3 (5), 9–14.

Rice, R. E. "The Future of Faculty Work and the Learning Community." Paper presented at the Transforming Campuses into Learning Communities Conference, Miami, Florida, January, 1998.

Schroeder, C. C. "New Students/New Learning Styles." *Change*, 1993, 25 (4), 21–26.

Schroeder, C. C. "Forging Educational Partnerships to Advance Student Learning." In G. S. Blimling and E. J. Whitt (eds.), *Good Practice in Student Affairs: Principles to Foster Student Learning.* San Francisco: Jossey-Bass, 1999.

Schroeder, C. C., and Hurst, J. "Designing Learning Environments that Integrate Curricular and Co-Curricular Experiences." *Journal of College Student Development*, 1996, 37, (2), 174–181.

Schroeder, C. C., Minor, F. D., and Tarkow, T. A. "Learning Communities: Partnerships Between Academic and Student Affairs." In J. H. Levine (ed.), *Learning Communities: New Structures, New Partnerships for Learning.* Columbia, S.C.: National Resource Center for the First Year Experience and Students in Transition, 1999, 59–69.

Schroeder, C. C., Nicholls, G. E., and Kuh, G. D. "Exploring the Rainforest: Testing Assumptions and Taking Risks." In G. D. Kuh (ed.), *Understanding Student Affairs Organizations.* New Directions for Student Services, no. 23. San Francisco: Jossey-Bass, 1983.

Senge, P. M. "The Leaders' New Work: Building Learning Organizations." *Sloan Management Review*, 1990, 32 (1), 7–23.

Seymour, D. *Once Upon a Campus: Lessons for Improving Quality and Productivity in Higher Education.* Phoenix: American Council on Education, 1995.

Terenzini, P. T., and Pascarella, E. T. "Living with Myths: Undergraduate Education in America." *Change*, 1994, 26 (1), 28–32.

Webster's New World College Dictionary (3rd Edition). New York: World, 1996.

Whitehead, A. N. *The Aims of Education and Other Essays.* New York: Free Press, 1929.

Whitt, E. J. "Some Propositions Worth Debating." *About Campus*, 1996, 1 (4), 31–32.

Wingspread Group. *An American Imperative: Higher Expectations for Higher Education.* Racine, Wisc.: Johnson Foundation, 1993.

Young, R. D. "Guiding Values in Philosophy." In S. R. Komives and D. B. Woodard (eds.), *Student Services: A Handbook for the Profession.* San Francisco: Jossey-Bass, 1996, 83–105.

Charles C. Schroeder is vice chancellor for student affairs at the University of Missouri-Columbia.

Service-learning programs that are grounded in collaboration between student affairs and academic affairs derive strength from the unique contributions of each partner.

Partnerships for Service Learning

Barbara Jacoby

Colleges and universities are called upon to renew their historic commitment to service while increasing the coherence and relevance of undergraduate education (Association of American Colleges, 1988; Bok, 1982, 1986; Boyer, 1994; Ehrlich, 1995; Wingspread Group on Higher Education, 1993). As a result, most institutions have developed, or are developing, opportunities for their students to engage in service learning.

It is unwise and inexpedient to propose a single blueprint or model for the development of service-learning programs. However, it is clear that most effective service-learning programs are based on partnerships between academic affairs and student affairs. Whatever the institutional location or reporting line of the program, service learning thrives on the expertise and experience of both academic affairs and student affairs. This chapter examines the nature of partnerships for service learning, profiles successful institutional partnerships, and provides guidance in establishing successful partnerships in a wide range of institutions.

Definition and Development of Service Learning

Service learning enables colleges and universities to enhance student learning and development while making unique contributions to their communities, the nation, and the world. Among frequently cited benefits to student participants in service learning are developing the habit of critical reflection; deepening comprehension of course content; integrating theory with practice; increasing understanding of the complex causes of social problems; strengthening one's sense of social responsibility; enhancing cognitive, personal, and spiritual development; heightening understanding of human difference and commonality; and sharpening abilities to solve problems creatively and to work collaboratively (Gray and others, 1996; Jacoby, 1996; Smith 1994).

Community benefits include new energy and assistance to broaden delivery of existing services or to begin new ones, fresh approaches to problem solving, access to institutional resources, and opportunities to participate in teaching and learning. Colleges and universities enjoy improved town-gown relationships, additional experiential learning settings for students, and new opportunities for faculty to orient their research and teaching in community contexts (Jacoby, 1996).

For the purposes of this chapter, *service learning* is defined as a form of experiential education in which students engage in activities that address human and community needs together with structured opportunities intentionally designed to promote student learning and development. Reflection and reciprocity are key concepts of service learning. The term *community* refers to local neighborhoods, the state, the nation, and the global community. The human and community needs that service learning addresses are those needs that are defined by the community (Jacoby, 1996).

As a form of experiential education, service learning is based on the pedagogical principle that learning and development do not necessarily result from experience itself but from reflection explicitly designed to foster learning and development. The other essential concept of service learning is reciprocity between the server and the person or group being served. "All parties in service-learning are learners and help determine what is to be learned. Both the server and those served teach, and both learn" (Kendall, 1990, p. 22). In service learning, those being served control the service provided. The needs of the community, as determined by its members, define what the service tasks will be. According to this definition, service learning is both curricular and cocurricular, because all learning does not occur in the classroom. Although some definitions of service learning insist that it must be integrated into the curriculum, student learning is indeed structured and facilitated by student affairs professionals, campus ministers, trained student leaders, and community members, in addition to faculty. Although the structure afforded by the curriculum (for example, class meetings, syllabi, assignments, grading, and credit) makes it easier to hold students accountable for achieving the desired outcomes of service learning, skillfully designed and implemented cocurricular experiences can yield rich learning and developmental outcomes as well (Jacoby, 1996).

A veritable explosion in the development of service-learning programs has occurred on college campuses in the 1990s. Organizations such as Campus Compact, the Campus Outreach Opportunity League, and the National Society for Experiential Education have been successful in promoting high-quality service learning through their constituencies of presidents, students, and practitioners, respectively. In addition, the conferences and publications of many higher education associations whose primary focus is not service learning or experiential education have featured large numbers of speakers and articles on service learning. Among these are the American Association of Higher Education, the Council of Independent Colleges, the United Negro College Fund, the American Association of Community Colleges, the National Association of Student Employment Administrators, the National Association of Student Personnel Administrators, the American College Personnel Association, the National Association of Campus Activities, and the Association of College Unions-International.

The federal government's interest in and support of service learning also increased substantially in the 1990s with the passage of the National and Community Service Trust Act of 1990 under President George Bush. After Bill Clinton's presidential campaign for a large-scale national service program, a long and heated congressional debate finally culminated in the passage of the National and Community Service Trust Act of 1993, the formation of the Corporation for National Service, and the Learn and Serve America programs. The Corporation's programs have given tremendous impetus to service learning in colleges and universities. Many institutions of higher education have entered into partnerships with community agencies and schools to engage college students in addressing a wide range of needs with funds from Ameri-Corps or Learn and Serve America grants (Jacoby, 1996). In other cases, service-learning programs have been started with institutional or private gift funds.

Service-learning programs are organizationally housed in many different locations. According to Campus Compact, the service-learning program reports to student affairs in 54 percent of its member institutions (Rothman, 1998); 23 percent are overseen by academic affairs. A smaller number of programs report directly to the president or provost (8 percent), a religious office (4 percent), a combination of locations cited above (5 percent), or other (4 percent) (Rothman, 1998).

Characteristics of Strong and Weak Service-Learning Programs

Service-learning programs exist at a wide range of levels of institutional commitment and support (Jacoby, 1996). Programs that are strong and central to their institutions share the following characteristics:

Service learning is prominently featured in the institutional mission and other key documents such as strategic plans and statements of goals. Funding is adequate and secure. The program receives permanent funding through the institution's budget and does not rely solely on grants or other "soft" money.

Policies explicitly support service learning. This can take many forms, including credit options for service learning, recognition of faculty service-learning involvement through the promotion and tenure process, and participation in service learning as a graduation requirement.

Institutional leadership is strongly committed to the program. This commitment can manifest itself in many ways, such as presidential speeches highlighting service learning, involvement of top administrators and faculty across functions and disciplines, and support of student leaders.

Student and faculty involvement is recognized and rewarded. Examples include institutional media regularly features service learning; student participation in service-learning is noted on transcripts; outstanding students receive service-learning scholarships, awards, and commencement regalia; and faculty are eligible for grants or release time for service-learning curriculum development and for awards for excellent teaching and research that involve service learning.

The program has strong external relationships. Community-based organizations, schools, other nonprofit organizations, businesses, and government agencies have lasting, consistent relationships of trust and mutual benefit with the institution regarding service learning.

Weak service-learning programs also have common characteristics:

- The program is on the periphery of institutional mission, planning, policies, and practices.
- Funding is inadequate and constantly in question.
- Those who are involved in the program feel marginal, isolated from the institutional mainstream.
- The program and its benefits are not widely understood on campus.
- External relationships are inconsistent and tenuous.

In general, programs housed in student affairs are more flexible in response to student needs and more open to student initiative and leadership than those located within academic affairs or other areas. However, they may not provide adequate opportunities for structured reflection, may risk giving too much emphasis to service and too little emphasis to learning, may lack academic credibility, and may have lower institutional priority and less stable funding. Programs primarily associated with academic affairs tend to be more connected with institutional mission, enable students to integrate disciplinary knowledge with practice, and are more likely to involve faculty in community-based research. At the same time, however, they risk placing too much emphasis on learning and too little on service and may be less likely to have solid administrative policies and procedures than those located in student affairs divisions.

No matter where service learning is located within the institution, service-learning programs benefit mightily from partnerships between student affairs and academic affairs. Each partner has at its disposal knowledge, connections, and resources that enable it to make unique and critical contributions to the development of high-quality service learning. Academic affairs leadership often results in service learning being viewed as more academically rigorous. Faculty may be more able to secure the support of senior administrators as well as to engage their faculty colleagues in service learning. Service-learning programs in academic affairs find it easier to modify and implement academic policy that supports service learning and to create mechanisms that reward faculty participation. Similarly, faculty development for service learning can be readily integrated into ongoing faculty development programs.

Student affairs professionals also have much to contribute to service learning. They possess knowledge of student development theory and learning styles and experience in group processes useful in the design and facilitation of reflection. In addition, student affairs practitioners are experienced in administration and logistics, including scheduling, transportation, risk management, and conflict mediation. They have networking and relationship-building skills. Many are active members of professional organizations, participants in workshops and listserv discussions, and readers of higher education publications that reflect cutting-edge concepts and practices related to service learning.

After a review of many service-learning programs at all types of institutions of higher education, I have selected several to describe here. Each was chosen because its success is largely a result of student affairs—academic affairs partnerships. These programs are located in student affairs, academic affairs, and a variety of other functions. The brief profiles of the programs and discussions of the nature of the partnerships on which they are based are intended to provide inspiration for the establishment and development of institutional partnerships for service learning.

Programs Located in Student Affairs

Although the majority of comprehensive service-learning offices are located in student affairs, most of those that involve students in both curricular and cocurricular service have developed strong relationships with academic affairs. Descriptions of several such programs follow.

University of Utah. According to its director, the Lowell Bennion Community Service Center at the University of Utah "has breached the wall between student affairs and academic affairs" (Fisher, 1998, p. 211). Indeed, the Bennion Center is well respected nationally because its "cocurricular and curricular service programs flourish side by side and continually grow in quality and quantity" (Fisher, 1998, p. 211). In fact, the Bennion Center's many curricular connections serve as often-replicated models. The center was born in 1985 when a Utah graduate offered the vice president for planning and budget a significant endowment to create a community service center similar to Stanford's. The vice president received endorsement for the center from the board of trustees, organized a board of advisors for the new center, developed its mission, and located it in student affairs. The center quickly established a student leadership model for cocurricular service projects, which continues to thrive today. Students direct over sixty ongoing service projects, which "provide the energy and foundation for all the cocurricular service activities at the center" (Fisher, 1998, p. 214). The student coordinators receive extensive training by participating in one of the center's two summer-of-service programs, as well as a fall orientation and regular meetings throughout the year.

In 1988, one year into the center's existence, the director hosted a focus group discussion to gather opinions from over forty faculty regarding faculty involvement in service learning. As a result, a faculty advisory committee was organized and a public service professorship award was created to enable faculty to receive release time to develop service-learning courses. The faculty committee "is still a key element in maintaining academic credibility for the center's curriculum-based programs" (Fisher, 1998, p. 219).

Another significant step in developing a partnership for curricular service learning occurred when the Bennion center staff saw a need to establish criteria for the designation of a course as service learning. The faculty advisory committee took on the task, and the resultant criteria have served well in the ongoing process of designating service-learning courses. The university offers eighty-five officially recognized service-learning courses in forty-five academic departments.

Other significant academic-student affairs partnerships include the service-learning scholars program, which recognizes six to eight students annually at commencement for significant community service, fifteen hours of service-learning courses, and a final integrative service project; a teaching assistant program that provides a trained student assistant to faculty members teaching a service-learning course for the first time; and a cutting-edge effort to institutionalize service learning within individual academic departments. With funds provided by the vice president for academic affairs, the vice president for student affairs, and the president, center staff invite academic departments to build service learning into their courses so that they will be taught as service-learning courses when any faculty member teaches them. This avoids one of the pitfalls of individual faculty development—if the faculty member leaves, the service-learning course is no longer taught. According to the Bennion Center's director, the partnership with academic affairs requires flexibility, financial support, and a spirit of collaboration on both sides.

Chandler-Gilbert Community College. The service-learning program at Chandler-Gilbert Community College (CGCC), at Maricopa Community College located in Chandler, Arizona, is housed in the office of student life. It provides comprehensive support for the growing number of faculty who teach service-learning courses. By making it as easy as possible for faculty to practice service learning, the director of student life explains that the faculty, in turn, ask the dean for additional staff and funding for the service-learning program. The CGCC service learning leadership team consists of the president, the deans of student services and instruction, the director and advisor in student life, the chair of the language and humanities division, and six faculty members. A stipended part-time faculty member also serves on the student life staff.

Over thirty courses require service learning in disciplines ranging from English, through biology and music, to education. The office of student life takes a more directive and hands-on approach to supporting service-learning courses than in many other models. Staff visit and evaluate every agency interested in being a service-learning site, approving only those that provide thorough training and supervision, are safe, and offer students generally good experiences.

Faculty members interested in teaching a service-learning course attend a workshop, and a student service learning assistant is then assigned to each class. The assistant places students in community service agencies related to the course, administers student paperwork (for example, liability forms, placement applications), arranges transportation, and tracks students' hours served at the sites. Student life staff monitor student placements, hold weekly meetings of service learning assistants, assist faculty as needed, and administer agency and student evaluations.

The office of student life also provides detailed instructions and evaluation criteria for service essays, which are short pieces to be written based on students' reflective journals and polished throughout the semester. The office publishes the essays in a bound book.

Chandler-Gilbert's service-learning program is an outstanding student affairs–academic affairs partnership that clearly articulates the benefits of service learning to students, faculty, and the community. In this vein, the service learning leadership team regularly asserts that the relevance of the service-learning experience "to student lives validates teaching and enhances learning" (Service Learning at Chandler-Gilbert Community College, undated brochure).

Georgetown University. The Volunteer and Public Service (VPS) Center at Georgetown University in Washington, D.C. "affirms the importance of integrating service with academics and personal action, providing a balanced approach to education" (Georgetown University Volunteer and Public Service Center, undated brochure). The center has long promoted and supported cocurricular service by linking individual students and student groups with community organizations and neighborhoods. The VPS Center director, a sociology faculty member who was a pioneer in teaching service-learning courses at Georgetown, provides faculty development and consultation for the design and teaching of new service-learning courses. The center director recently has worked with faculty colleagues to create the Faculty Center for the Study and Support of Service Learning, of which he serves as associate director. The new center, directed by an English faculty member, is the result of a faculty-driven initiative. It will provide release time and other assistance to faculty in developing service-learning courses.

Georgetown was one of the first universities to create a fourth-credit option program for service learning, recently renamed the Service-Learning Credit. The Service-Learning Credit program is administered through the VPS Center and funded by student affairs. Students may arrange with any faculty member to earn an additional credit in any three-credit course by completing forty hours of community service and meeting the goals set forth in a learning contract signed by the professor, the student's home college dean's office, and the VPS Center. The VPS Center assists students in identifying service sites, coordinates required guided-reflection sessions, and contacts the site to ensure that students meet their service commitments. Written reflection essays are submitted to the faculty member, who assigns the grade for the Service-Learning Credit. The Service-Learning Credit program is an excellent example of a student affairs–academic affairs partnership in which VPS Center staff and faculty each assume roles for which they are uniquely suited.

Other Models. Another model is the Haas Center for Public Service at Stanford University. They have often formed faculty steering committees to help design curricular service-learning projects and to work on the institutional level as advocates for service learning. In a different model, the Community Service Office at Macalester College in St. Paul, Minnesota, has initiated an action research project in a local neighborhood regarding high turnover in the elementary school and its relationship to housing stock, jobs, and crime. The project is led by the director of community service, a faculty member, and the former mayor of St. Paul, who is a visiting faculty member at Macalester.

The Center for Community Service at Ohio University is also housed in student affairs with close ties to student activities, where it has its roots. The service-learning initiative began in 1992 as a partnership with University College, the entry and general education college and home to the Center for Teaching Excellence. Each year, the partners seek funding together and cosponsor a service-learning institute for faculty.

At Elon College in North Carolina, the Kernodle Center for Service Learning is located in student life and houses both the curricular service-learning program and Elon Volunteers, a student-run volunteer program. The college offers the Elon Experiences Transcript, which documents student participation in experiential education. The college's general studies program has an experiential education requirement; other programs strongly encourage it. In addition to providing many additional forms of support for both curricular and cocurricular service learning, the center validates service experiences for transcript notation and administers the Service Learning Workbook, which, once completed, fulfills the general studies program's experiential learning requirement.

Programs Housed in Academic Affairs

Of the service-learning programs located within academic affairs, those that are most comprehensive tend to enjoy strong, positive relationships with student affairs. At Azusa Pacific University in Azusa, California, where the service-learning office is located in academic affairs, students are required to perform 120 hours of community service to graduate. The office works closely with the volunteer center, housed in student affairs, to incorporate the volunteer projects into the classroom. The director of the Office of Community Service Learning attends meetings of both student affairs directors and the faculty development committee. Volunteer Action Services at the University of Montana in Missoula is sponsored by the Davidson Honors College. It supports and promotes both volunteerism and curricular service learning. At Augsburg College in Minneapolis, experiential education has long been institutionalized in its mission and programs. Its service-learning program is overseen by a faculty member who reports to the academic dean and the vice president of academic affairs. It evolved with the support of a college-wide advisory committee, consisting of student leaders, faculty members, and the assistant to the president for community affairs, with the chair from the student affairs division. Its partnerships with student affairs feature a close working relationship between the service-learning coordinator and residence hall staff to create service-learning projects for each residential unit.

At North Carolina Central University, a historically black liberal arts institution, the Community Service Program (CSP) was developed by a tenured full professor of history and a planning team consisting of faculty and student leaders. Its director explains that the program's key objective to promote an ethic of service has led to "a natural alliance among the office of student affairs, the student government association, and the CSP" (Jones, 1998, p. 115). Detailed descriptions of other examples of this model are provided in the following paragraphs.

George Mason University. The Center for Service and Leadership, the service-learning program at George Mason University in Fairfax, Virginia, is housed in an academic unit called New Century College. New Century College's mission is "to provide a learning environment that integrates interdisciplinary knowledge with workplace and lifelong learning skills" (George Mason University, "Learning Communities: Your First Year," undated brochure). New Century College requires that students take an active role in developing eight competencies: communication, critical thinking and analysis, problem solving, valuing, social interaction, global perspective, effective citizenship, and aesthetic response. It offers highlights such as small groups of students and faculty working together; integration of disciplines such as psychology and marketing, computers and art, and scientific writing; and extensive opportunities for internships, co-ops, study abroad, and service learning.

New Century College enjoys many mutually beneficial partnerships with student affairs. For example, the director of service learning teaches a two-credit course on special events leadership, which engages students in service projects for on- and off-campus programs, such as Alternative Spring Break, International Week, and a technology camp for young women. Likewise, many student services staff teach the University 101 freshman transition course, some sections of which involve service learning. In support of other service-learning courses, student services staff provide service-learning placements or personal assistance to students who confront difficult issues at their service sites. In one instance, the sexual assault services office worked with students involved in service learning as part of an eight-credit learning community on violence and gender. As at many other institutions, these partnerships often arise informally and are not officially documented. Nonetheless, they are important and effective means of collaboration and support for service learning.

California State University, Monterey Bay. California State University, Monterey Bay, was founded in 1995 to address two complementary needs: an influx of new college students from the California school system and the need for a new community support system to address the massive loss of jobs after the closing of a nearby military base. Its founding vision statement articulates that the university is "framed by substantive commitment to a multilingual, multicultural, intellectual community distinguished by partnerships with existing institutions, both public and private, and by cooperative agreements which enable students, faculty, and staff to cross institutional boundaries for innovative instruction, broadly defined scholarly creative activity, and coordinated community service" (Rothman, 1998, p. 84).

Service learning is incorporated thoroughly into the curriculum. All students are required to take an introductory course on community participation and at least one service-learning course related to their major. Every service-learning course is developed with input from community members and team-taught by interdisciplinary groups of faculty members and representatives of community organizations.

Although the Service Learning Institute is situated in academic affairs, it works closely with student affairs to create the University Service Advocates (USA) program. The USA are student leaders who are "a critical piece of the service-learning process" (Seth Pollack, personal communication, 1998). They work with faculty in curriculum development, support community partners, and lead cocurricular service activities. The student affairs-academic affairs partnership for service-learning at CSU-MB is embodied in the title of one of the program's key staff members: coordinator of student leadership and faculty support.

Portland State University. As at California State University, Monterey Bay, service-learning at Portland State University (PSU) is rooted firmly in the institution's commitment to its community. In the case of PSU, the service-learning program is more the result of an institution-wide strategic reorganization of its curriculum and its administrative structure than of partnerships between discrete student affairs and academic affairs units. The campus is located in the downtown area, surrounded by many district neighborhoods with varying needs. The majority of PSU's students come from these neighborhoods. In 1992, university leaders responded to community needs, financial constraints, and growing concerns about student learning and retention by creating a service-learning program that is "comprehensive, integrated throughout the curriculum, and a primary learning experience for students from the time they arrive on campus until they graduate" (Driscoll, 1998, p. 151).

In developing its comprehensive service-learning design, PSU looked at its student characteristics, its faculty characteristics, its institutional history, and the needs of its urban setting. Student characteristics were examined in terms of Astin's work in which he identifies factors that have a negative effect on general education outcomes (1992). Factors most pertinent among PSU students are living at home and commuting, working full time, and off-campus employment.

To bring about necessary change, PSU developed a strategic plan that resulted in the redesign of administrative services by clustering related units, redesigning campus operations, and introducing new technologies. Three key events served to integrate service learning into the new comprehensive institutional design: the implementation of a new general education curriculum that connects academic content with community service in many ways, receipt of a Learn and Serve America grant, and the start of the Center for Academic Excellence. The Center is staffed by a director of teaching and learning excellence, a director of community/university partnerships, and a faculty assessment team. With the support of the Center and its staff, the institution continues to develop multiple forms of service learning to "ensure that all students will have the opportunity to learn from the community and to experience participation in community work" (Driscoll, 1998, p. 166). Without institution-wide collaboration, this goal could never be achieved.

Programs in Other Institutional Locations

Most service-learning programs that are located wholly in neither academic affairs nor student affairs enjoy some kind of joint-reporting structure that ensures a high level of collaboration. For example, the service-learning position at Gonzaga University originally reported to the volunteer services office in student life and then to both volunteer services and the faculty service-learning committee. Funding for the position was initially provided by student life. Because the service-learning coordinator primarily serves faculty, the director of the volunteer services office and the faculty committee wrote a proposal to request that academic affairs split the costs associated with the position with student life. The academic affairs vice president accepted the proposal, and the service-learning position remains the only position funded in this way at Gonzaga.

Similarly, the director of the Leadership Development Institute at the University of Detroit Mercy, which provides academic support for service learning, is the only unit at the institution that reports to both the vice president for academic affairs and the vice president for student affairs.

At Cornell College in Iowa, the director of volunteer services is a part-time faculty member who reports to the associate academic dean and the dean of students. She also reports informally to the president, who has a great interest in service. The director of volunteer services coordinates both curricular and cocurricular activities.

The director of public service at Hobart and William Smith, a private liberal arts college in upstate New York, reports to the dean of the college. He spends half his time working with student affairs staff on cocurricular activities and the other half with academic affairs, working on curricular programs. As an outgrowth of this partnership, the career services center in student affairs has partnered with academic affairs to develop an intensive internship program.

The office for service learning and volunteer programs at Colorado State University was originally established in 1975 as the office of community services to coordinate cocurricular service projects. It reported to the vice president for student affairs until it received a grant from the Corporation for National Service to develop a program to integrate service into the curriculum. As the grant funding declined each year, the funding for the Service Integration Project (SIP) was picked up by academic affairs. The SIP is currently a joint project of student affairs and academic affairs, maintaining its formal reporting line to the vice president for student affairs but receiving 70 percent of its funding and much counsel and direction from the provost.

The SIP provides a broad range of services to faculty, including individual assistance with site selection, syllabus revision, student orientation, reflection activities, and evaluation; educational seminars and support to attend service-learning conferences; minigrants; a resource library; a service-learning newsletter and listserv; and recognition and awards.

At Niagara University in New York, 75 percent of the students participate in service learning. A legacy of St. Vincent de Paul, community service has been an integral part of Niagara's mission for over thirty years. Its service-learning program began as a partnership between campus ministry, housed in student affairs, and faculty interested in service learning. Learn and Serve Niagara, which has become the umbrella office for all curricular and cocurricular service activities, reports directly to the president. It received funding from the Corporation for National Service in 1994.

Service-learning courses are now offered in every college and in almost every academic department at Colorado State University. In addition to substantial growth in student involvement in cocurricular service, the university expects that service-learning course offerings will increase by at lease four courses per year, thus eventually allowing every student the opportunity to participate in academic service learning.

Elmhurst College (Illinois) opened the Center for Professional Excellence in 1997 to integrate programs that cut across academic and student affairs, including career services, international education, and service learning. First-year students are invited to submit an essay in the form of a letter to the first significant person they met at the college in which they describe their life ten years after graduation. The content of the essays then guides the creation of each student's personal and professional development plan, which encompasses curricular and cocurricular interests. Also during their freshman year, students shadow professionals in their work environments and use self-assessment instruments to better understand their own life and career goals.

The coordinator of service learning, who also is a professor of nursing, offers many different types of service-learning activities "to develop behaviors reflecting responsible citizenship based on humane values and mutual respect for others," a goal taken from the college's mission statement (Elmhurst College, *President's Annual Report* 1996–1997, no page number). Service learning can be a one-time experience, integrated into a course, offered as an independent study, and, in the future, linked with international study.

Case Study: Partnership for Service Learning at the University of Maryland

Although the service-learning partnerships described above are intended to provoke insight and guidance, the case study of the ongoing development of service learning at the University of Maryland is offered here to help readers identify and understand processes and politics in the evolution of any partnership between academic affairs and student affairs. The details of the case relate specifically to Maryland, but the complexities, tensions, and triumphs are common to many service-learning programs. As a land-grant institution, the flagship of the University System of Maryland, and a Carnegie I research university, the University of Maryland, College Park, has a tripartite mission: to provide high quality education, to advance knowledge through research, and to provide service for the State of Maryland and its citizens. Some individuals have developed long-standing, mutually beneficial relationships with communities and have engaged students in service learning. Yet until recently, they did so without the assistance of a university office whose purpose was to support such relationships and activities.

On July 1, 1992, the office of commuter affairs (now commuter affairs and community service, CACS) was given responsibility for community service and was asked by the vice president for student affairs, to whom it reports, to develop and promote opportunities for all students to participate in meaningful community service. The office of commuter affairs was selected because of its twenty-year history of providing high-quality services and programs for the more than 75 percent of UM students who commute to the campus, its strong advocacy on behalf of students, and its solid foundation of collaborative relationships with other campus departments, student organizations, and external agencies.

The new function, community service programs, began with an allocation of only a one half-time (ten hours per week) graduate assistant and $10,000 in operating funds. Additional support was provided by the director and associate director and by reallocation of other office funds and student positions. From the very beginning, staff placed a high priority on building relationships with the curriculum and with faculty, realizing that to do otherwise would doom the program to be marginal, rather than central, at the university. The fledgling program's first objectives were to create a database of community service agencies and opportunities, develop relationships with agencies where students had or were likely to have good experiences, promote and enhance service learning in the university's honors programs, seek faculty with interest or experience in service learning, and create printed materials that connected academic majors to community service opportunities. Another of the early orders of business was to convince the president to join Campus Compact, the organization of presidents who commit their institutions to community service.

In 1994, these efforts were rewarded and encouraged when the provost and the vice president for student affairs provided one year of funding for a half-time coordinator of service learning. The request for the position was made by the director of commuter affairs and the dean for undergraduate studies. The coordinator would work with faculty members by providing them with sample course syllabi, connections with community service agencies, and other technical assistance in designing service-learning courses.

When the funding for the half-time position for coordinator of service learning expired after one year, the director and dean requested continued funding and expansion of the position to full time. The provost denied the request, stating that it was somewhat "premature." He added that he would reconsider the request in a year if substantial faculty support for service learning could be demonstrated.

Based on the provost's instructions, the director worked with Campus Compact to host a regional institute on integrating service with academic study at UM. Eight teams of faculty and staff, representing a wide range of institutional types, attended the institute. Maryland sent two teams. One team comprised faculty and staff of College Park Scholars, a program for outstanding first- and second-year students; the other included faculty interested in service learning, the past chair of the campus senate, the executive assistant to the vice president for student affairs, and the director of commuter affairs. The teams developed detailed action plans, one for the integration of service learning into the College Park Scholars program and one for the inclusion of service learning in the university's strategic plan, which was being developed at that time. Both action plans were implemented. The strategic plan adopted in March 1996 contains the language drafted by the institute team: "Support efforts to engage students, faculty, and staff in service-learning opportunities that enhance the academic experience and improve the quality of life for the citizens of the State" (*Charting a Path to Excellence: The Strategic Plan for the University of Maryland at College Park*, p. 22). This team also recommended the formation of a service-learning advisory group, consisting of faculty currently practicing service learning, influential faculty who are unfamiliar or only slightly familiar with service learning, and key student affairs leaders.

The service-learning advisory group met through the fall of 1996 and in January 1997 provided a list of suggestions to the provost and the vice president for student affairs. The advisory group recommended that the university embrace service learning as an integral part of a University of Maryland education and offer students a wide range of opportunities for involvement in service learning, both curricular and cocurricular, throughout their college experience. They also recommended the hiring of a full-time coordinator of service learning to provide faculty development and additional technical assistance to integrate service learning into the curriculum.

Based on these recommendations, CACS received funds to hire a full-time coordinator of service learning in 1997. Since then, several key initiatives have been put in place. The coordinator has created a sophisticated database of faculty and service-learning courses and assembled a comprehensive library of readings, syllabi, reflection exercises, and other resources to assist faculty. She has developed a solid working relationship with the Center for Teaching Excellence, a relationship that has yielded many substantial benefits. Each issue of the Teaching Center's newsletter contains an article on service learning written by the coordinator, and its innovative instructional grant program now includes grants for service learning funded jointly by the Center and CACS. In 1998, two grants were awarded, one to support a service-learning course in Vietnam and the other for the development of a departmental Center for Teaching Excellence in American Studies with a heavy focus on service learning.

The coordinator for service learning also has connected UM faculty with local and national faculty development opportunities. A mechanical engineering faculty member participated in the March 1998 National Service-Learning Institute for Engineering, Mathematics, and Science Faculty sponsored by Campus Compact. Three faculty members participated in the DC Faculty Fellows program that met during the spring 1998 semester to develop service-learning courses to be taught during the 1998–1999 academic year. Faculty whose involvement in service learning is significant are recognized by letters from the president, subscriptions to service-learning publications, and nomination for national awards.

In addition to the primarily curricular focus of the coordinator of service learning, the community service programs unit of CACS has increased its support of both curricular and cocurricular service. Two graduate assistants coordinate a wide range of services and programs, including a database of over 800 community service agencies with personalized search capabilities that is available on the World Wide Web, a monthly community service newsletter with a mailing list of over 1,300, a computer mail reflector that provides weekly and emergency updates of current opportunities and needs, presentations to numerous groups and classes, community service fairs, recognition of outstanding student involvement in community service, orientation sessions for new students, intensive support to student organizations, and a host of publications.

What lies ahead for service learning at the University of Maryland? The director and associate director of CACS, the coordinator of service learning, and other community service programs staff will continue to work together to shape the direction of both curricular and cocurricular service at the University of Maryland. Questions yet to be resolved include: To what extent should the staff support cocurriculur community service by fraternities and sororities and residence hall groups, rather than increasing services to faculty teaching service-learning courses? Should curricular and cocurricular service be focused on particular communities or issues (for example, literacy or homelessness)? How can student affairs and academic affairs work together to continue to integrate service learning into the life and work of the university?

Short-term goals are to produce a faculty handbook for service learning, increase services and support to student groups in designing and implementing high-quality service-learning experiences, pilot an undergraduate teaching assistant program for service learning, and seek private funding for the development of service learning. Toward this last goal, the vice president for student affairs has identified the creation of a comprehensive center for service learning as one of his division's priorities for the institution's current capital campaign.

Conclusion

Whatever the extent and nature of the partnerships that undergird an institution's service-learning program, there is little doubt that the benefits they supply far outweigh the frustrations and problems that might arise. Academic affairs–student affairs partnerships combine academic rigor with student leadership, faculty development with student development, and faculty disciplinary expertise with student affairs professionals' administrative experience. The financial burden and responsibility for high-quality outcomes are shared. Some service-learning partnerships flourish within traditional institutional organizational boundaries; others forge new organizational patterns that lead to further collaboration. In the long run, partnerships that enjoy the support of both academic and student affairs leaders also find it easier to obtain the endorsement of presidents and governing boards. Service-learning partnerships will continue to thrive because the powerful combination of service and learning will continue to inspire educators from all walks of academic life to join together with students and communities in the spirit of partnership for the common good.

References

Association of American Colleges. *A New Vitality in General Education.* Washington, D.C.: Association of American Colleges, 1988.

Astin, A. W. "What Really Matters in General Education: Provocative Findings from a National Study of Student Outcomes." *Perspectives,* 1992, 22 (11), 23–46.

Bok, D. *Beyond the Ivory Tower: Social Responsibilities of the Modern University.* Cambridge, Mass.: Harvard University Press, 1982.

Bok, D. *Higher Learning.* Cambridge, Mass.: Harvard University Press, 1986.

Boyer, E. L. "Creating the New American College." *Chronicle of Higher Education,* Mar. 9, 1994, p. 48.

Driscoll, A. "Comprehensive Design of Community Service: New Understandings, Options, and Vitality in Student Learning at Portland State University." In E. Zlotkowski (ed.), *Successful Service-Learning Programs: New Models of Excellence in Higher Education.* Bolton, Mass.: Anker, 1998.

Ehrlich, T. "Taking Service Seriously." *American Association of Higher Education Bulletin,* 1995, 47 (7), 8–10.

Fisher, I. S. "We Make the Road by Walking: Building Service-Learning in and out of the Curriculum at the University of Utah." In E. Zlotkowski (ed.), *Successful Service-Learning Programs: New Models of Excellence in Higher Education.* Bolton, Mass.: Anker, 1998.

Gray, M. J., and others. *Evaluation of Learn and Serve America, Higher Education: First Year Report, Volume 1.* Washington, D.C.: Rand Institute on Education and Training, 1996.

Jacoby, B. *Service Learning in Higher Education: Concepts and Practices.* San Francisco: Jossey-Bass, 1996.

Jones, B. W. "Rediscovering Our Heritage: Community Service and the Historically Black University." In E. Zlotkowski (ed.), *Successful Service-Learning Programs: New Models of Excellence in Higher Education.* Bolton, Mass.: Anker, 1998.

Kendall, J. C. "Combining Service and Learning: An Introduction." In J. C. Kendall (ed.), *Combining Service and Learning: A Resource Book for Community and Public Service,* Vol. 1. Raleigh, N.C.: National Society for Experimental Education, 1990.

Rothman, M. (ed.). *Service Matters.* Providence, R.I.: Campus Compact, 1998.

Smith, M. W. "Community Service Learning: Striking the Chord of Citizenship." *Michigan Journal of Community Service Learning,* 1994, *1* (1), 37–43.

Wingspread Group on Higher Education. *An American Imperative: Higher Expectations for Higher Education.* Racine, Wisc.: Johnson Foundation, 1993.

BARBARA JACOBY is director of commuter affairs and community service, affiliate associate professor of college student personnel, and instructor of French at the University of Maryland, College Park.

This chapter describes an innovative and effective partnership for promoting student success through the creation of residential learning communities called Freshman Interest Groups.

Freshman Interest Groups: Partnerships for Promoting Student Success

Charles C. Schroeder, Frankie D. Minor, Theodore A. Tarkow

This chapter describes an innovative and effective partnership for promoting student success: residential learning communities called Freshman Interest Groups (FIGs). The chapter is structured according to the following questions: How did this collaboration get started? How was the need for such collaboration determined? What form did the collaboration take? Who provided the leadership and the resources? What did the campus do? What problems were encountered? How was the program evaluated? The last section provides recommendations, implications, and conclusions for institutions seeking to create learning communities through partnerships between academic affairs and student affairs.

How Did This Collaboration Get Started?

Collaborative partnerships between academic affairs and student affairs often have multiple origins, and it is not uncommon for them to be forged from "triggering" opportunities. The FIGs at the University of Missouri–Columbia (MU), a research I university, were a response to several events occurring close together in time. First, in 1992, MU hired a new chancellor, who immediately established a goal of "recapturing the public's trust" by reinvigorating undergraduate education. The chancellor knew that the research mission of the institution would not be supported unless important external constituents saw tangible, concrete evidence of a renewed commitment to high-quality undergraduate education. Also in 1992, the university chose to become a "selective" institution and thereby agreed to meet two performance standards established by the state's Coordinating Board for Higher Education: (1) a freshman to sophomore retention rate of 85 percent, with all students completing 24 credit hours with a 2.0 GPA or better, and (2) a six-year graduation rate of 65 percent.

In addition to these challenges, residence hall occupancy at MU had declined from 6,200 to 4,100 and three of the nineteen residence halls had been closed. Student dissatisfaction with residential living led to few students choosing to return to the halls as sophomores or juniors.

Finally, many external constituents, particularly legislators, high school guidance counselors, and parents, perceived the university as a large, bureaucratic, and uncaring place that was uninterested in undergraduates. These issues created the opportunity for a collaborative partnership between academic affairs and student affairs to reinvigorate undergraduate education at MU.

How Was the Need for Such Collaboration Determined?

Shortly after the arrival of the new chancellor, a new vice chancellor for student affairs was hired. This individual had a particular interest in residential education and was committed to addressing problems associated with low occupancy and student dissatisfaction in the halls. Prior to his arrival, the vice chancellor had participated in an American Association for Higher Education (AAHE) Assessment Forum program on FIGs that had been implemented at the Universities of Oregon and Washington. Recognizing the substantial impact these learning communities had on freshman achievement and retention, the new vice chancellor was intrigued with the possibility of transforming the commuter-based program used at Washington and Oregon to a residential model.

At the same time, the associate dean of the College of Arts and Sciences was interested in implementing a FIG program for another reason: expanding early registration opportunities for incoming freshmen. Traditionally, freshmen registered for their courses during one of fifteen summer orientation sessions scheduled in June and July. As a result, the associate dean was rarely able to predict demand for required general education courses. The FIGs model presented multiple opportunities for solving this institutional challenge. Finally, a senior faculty member, the chair of biological sciences, was interested in creating learning communities, primarily as a way to help students make intellectual connections among courses during their freshman year and to sustain student interest in the sciences.

Through the efforts of these leaders, the initial collaboration was launched to create residential learning communities that would accomplish the following objectives: (1) substantially enhance academic achievement, retention, and educational attainment for freshmen, (2) make the large campus feel small by creating peer reference groups for new students, (3) integrate curricular and cocurricular experiences through the development of a seamless learning environment, (4) provide a means for admitted students to register early for their fall classes, and (5) encourage faculty to integrate ideas, content, writing, and research from their disciplines, thereby enhancing general education outcomes for students.

The learning communities, or FIGs, are small groups of students (usually fifteen to twenty), each of which takes three core, general education courses that address a particular theme. FIG students are assigned to the same residence hall community and coenroll in the same sections of three core courses as well as Interdisciplinary Studies 1: Freshman Pro-seminar. Each FIG has a peer advisor, an advanced undergraduate student who helps students make the adjustment to college and who usually lives in the residence hall with FIG members. Each FIG also has a cofacilitator, a faculty or staff member who serves as an additional resource for the FIG. The cofacilitator and peer advisor teach their FIG pro-seminar, a one-credit class that covers essential skills for success at college and explores academic issues related to the FIG theme.

What Form Did the Collaboration Take?

Although key administrators were committed to this project, they recognized that a broader range of highly invested institutional partners would be necessary for this project to succeed. Essential offices, departments, and individuals were identified and invited to assist with the initial planning and development. The large planning group included key faculty from selected departments, students, and leaders from registration, admissions, general education program, Learning Center, academic advising, and residential life.

In addition to identifying the goals and core objectives, the planning group engaged in extensive discussions about the process and methods that would be used to achieve the objectives. It became apparent that to be successful, students' experiences must transcend departmental and divisional boundaries. This was both a challenge and an opportunity, in that institutional structures and procedures usually are "owned" by a specific office or department, and operational and political boundaries often inhibit collaboration. Therefore, the collaborating partners had to demonstrate flexibility and creative thinking, as well as change and compromise, when determining the processes and experiences that would become core elements of the FIGs program.

Who Provided the Leadership and the Resources? Accomplishing the goals of the FIGs program—to connect students' in- and out-of-class learning and social experiences—required conceptual leadership and logistic coordination. In selecting partners to represent various departments, it was critical to identify individuals who, by virtue of their position and their predisposition, supported the project's objectives and had the authority to make decisions, commit resources, and affect change in their areas. In many situations, these were directors, but assistant directors or management staff who understood the finer details of their operations also were included. The associate dean for arts and sciences and the director of residential life provided primary leadership in this large planning group. The vice chancellor for student affairs served as the champion and advocate for the FIGs program at senior administrative levels within the campus.

Although a large committee expands investment in an initiative, it also can inhibit significant and timely progress. In response to this concern, a subset of the planning group, nicknamed the FIGs core group, was selected to meet weekly to work out most operational and implementation details. The large planning group was reconvened periodically to hear updates and discuss broader issues. The core group included the associate dean, the residential life director, an academic advisor, a Learning Center director (who held a faculty appointment), a residence hall coordinator, a graduate student FIGs coordinator, two students, and a residential life staff member responsible for student learning initiatives in the department. After four years, the core group still meets weekly, and the larger planning team receives updates throughout the year.

An essential aspect of the FIGs program's first year was the commitment of the associate dean and residential life director to devote their own time, as well as staff time and financial resources, to make the program work. Costs were split as evenly as possible, based on a logical assignment of costs. Small faculty stipends came from the academic budget, for example, and student staff stipends were paid from residential life. As the effectiveness of the program was demonstrated, the chancellor, vice chancellor for student affairs, and provost agreed to fund all program costs.

What Did the Campus Do? Although the allocation of financial resources was a strong indicator of commitment, perhaps even more profound was the willingness to alter current operating procedures significantly to accommodate the integration between the living and learning experiences for students. This included identifying sections of general education and departmental classes that would constitute the three courses in each FIG and holding spaces in these classes. New students also were assigned to these spaces in the spring, well ahead of the summer registration and orientation period for all other new students. Spaces were identified on residence hall floors, and FIG students were assigned to them, foregoing the computerized assignment process that placed students in all other spaces weeks later. FIG students were thus given priority in class and residence hall assignments over other students. This did not, however, result in any significant complaints and was endorsed by the student newspaper, which is known for its criticism of special practices and administrative decisions.

What Problems Were Encountered?

As with any new initiative, some trials and errors were necessary to refine the program. However, most of the adjustments did not affect any of the essential elements or objectives of the program directly, and the challenges encountered can be grouped into three categories: communication, transition issues, and insufficient anticipation. The challenges we encountered were not, for the most part, due to the significant amount of collaboration the FIGs program required.

Instead, the difficulties we faced actually were ameliorated because of the high level of cooperation and commitment among the partners.

Communication. Development of the FIGs program began with discussions in November 1994, and the program was implemented in the fall semester, 1995, with twenty-one FIGs and 225 participants. This implementation schedule prevented the inclusion of the program in any institutional recruitment and promotional materials; however, this approach did present an opportunity for new methods, including a direct mailing to all admitted students prior to mailing of FIG materials and the distribution of a letter to admitted students and their parents from the chancellor to build anticipation and support for the program.

Because admitted students received information from a variety of sources, a need emerged to provide answers to some questions and clarify misconceptions. For example, since MU offers both an engineering learning community and an engineering FIG, students would inquire, Which is better? Other typical questions included, Can a student be in a FIG and still live with a requested roommate who is not in a FIG? Isn't the pro-seminar just a study hall? When answers to questions such as these come from different sources, they can inadvertently be inappropriate or confusing. Therefore, we recognized early in the process that clear, effective, and coordinated communication must come from a single source whenever possible. The FIGs core group, most often represented by the associate dean and residential life director, became the primary resources for providing information to the other sources that students contacted with questions. The decision that both the associate dean and residential life director would sign all FIG-related communications underscored the collaborative nature of the program.

Transition. Other challenges arose as the program became established and expanded rapidly. The success of an individual FIG is due in large part to the efforts of the student peer advisor (PA). This position appeals to students of very strong academic ability (the average grade point average of PAs usually exceeds 3.70) who typically are not attracted to traditional student paraprofessional positions (for example, resident assistants). Because most PAs live on the floor with their FIG students, issues arose regarding roles and responsibilities. Whom do students contact with a concern if they are in a FIG—the PA or the community advisor (CA)? Is educational programming the responsibility of the PA or CA? Do PAs attend the hall staff meetings? Does the hall coordinator supervise or evaluate the PAs? These questions and many others led to another collaborative effort when residential life staff and the FIGs coordinator designed an integrated training program for CAs and PAs to be implemented immediately prior to the start of the fall semester. Joint training resulted in less confusion and greater collaboration.

In 1998 over 900 students participated in sixty-one FIGs, a number that represents almost one-quarter of the entering freshman class. In addition to linking the FIGs with other residential learning communities, new strategies have been implemented to address some space challenges. These included distributing FIG students within a building, rather than on the same floor.

Another strategy assigned students to the hall they requested and then established a FIG community "virtually" through e-mail, chat rooms, and other technology, or through shared service learning projects. The results of these two arrangements differed considerably. FIG students distributed widely do not enjoy the same benefits or satisfaction as those who live together, unless their "linked" learning community also covered more than one floor. The virtual communities seemed to work, however, offering the degree of independence and community these students sought.

The program has encountered some challenges that have both tested and strengthened the collaboration between the academic and student affairs partners. As the success of the program has been demonstrated and broadly communicated, the demand for the program from students, parents, administrators, and even faculty has increased, thus prompting some concern about losing quality in an effort to provide quantity. Access to the classes and residence hall spaces for nonparticipants is an issue that unites both academic and housing administrators. An unintended yet positive outcome has been a keener understanding of the operational and logistical issues associated with course and residence hall assignments by the partners who do not bear primary responsibility for each. This development has led to a greater level of collaboration and compromise, thereby insuring the quality of the program.

Insufficient Anticipation. In spite of the planning, foresight, and experience of the members of the large planning team and core group, the program still encountered some challenges that were unanticipated or underestimated. In recruitment materials for the first year of the program, students were told that their initial housing preferences would be used only if they were not assigned to a FIG. Otherwise, where they lived was dictated by the location of their FIG. However, as demand for the program was unpredictable, students were not told where a FIG would be housed in order to allow staff maximum flexibility after applications were received. Although there were spaces for 420 students, only 225 elected to participate. In subsequent surveys and focus groups, students stated that where they live is very important, and most were unwilling to risk uncertainty in their housing assignment. Now FIG descriptions include the list of courses that constitute the FIG, its residence hall location, and whether it is part of a theme-oriented learning community (for example, women in engineering).

Collaboration with the Honors College yielded several honors sections of FIGs for students with strong academic skills. However, the growing number of students with advance placement or college credit was not sufficiently anticipated and the demand for these FIGs exceeded supply. In addition, students occasionally dropped classes that composed the FIG during summer registration or at add/drop periods during the start of the semester. Some did this to get class sections that met later in the day, or they requested the FIG as a "back door" into a particular residence hall. As a result of these problems, the program now permits students to participate in a FIG as long as they share two of the three classes in common with their fellow FIG students. If a student drops more than one FIG class, she is removed from the FIG and her housing assignment is changed.

Although the above examples did not profoundly affect the collaboration among different areas of campus, some issues highlighted the need for working together and provided some challenges to doing so. The pro-seminar was designed to be cotaught by the peer advisor and faculty cofacilitator. However, implementation of design revealed two concerns. First, many faculty were unaccustomed to "sharing the stage" in the classroom. Any involvement they may have had with instructors usually was limited to graduate teaching assistants whom they supervised. The pro-seminar was intended to be a true partnership between a talented undergraduate and a faculty member, and some conflicts over roles and responsibilities arose.

Second, the curriculum of the pro-seminar blended academic issues related to the FIG theme and transition issues related to success in the freshman year (time management, study skills, diversity, and so on). Faculty were familiar with the former, but typically much less so with the latter. These two concerns provided yet another collaborative opportunity for the FIGs core group. The academic partners were well acquainted with faculty culture, pedagogy, and curriculum development. The student affairs partners were well versed in the success-skills content areas, as well as conflict mediation and training issues. The combination of these talents resulted in successful strategies to develop a curriculum that is both standardized and flexible, resolve conflicts, and provide training to faculty and student staff on teaching approaches and content areas unfamiliar to each group.

Sharing classes with a small group of students with whom they lived was, for most students, one of the most attractive and beneficial aspects of the FIGs program, for both academic and social reasons. This led to an interest in coenrolling for common courses in the second semester as well as the first. However, registration procedures in place at that time assigned registration dates to students based on class rank and student number. Also, internal political sensitivities discouraged giving some continuing students preferential registration priorities over others. Despite these obstacles, many FIG students attempted to register together for sections of classes with varying results. In the third year of the program, the FIGs core group identified some FIGs related to academic majors who followed very predictable and sometimes unyielding course-sequencing formats (for example, engineering, life sciences, or nursing). By collaborating with these academic departments and the registrar's office, some of FIGs were given the opportunity to coenroll for two courses in the second semester; this was facilitated by the recognition that most students would be taking the same courses anyway. Over 90 percent of the students who were given this opportunity elected to do so. Based on this interest, and with the cooperation from academic departments, all FIG students now have the opportunity to coenroll for the second semester.

Structural and Organizational Obstacles. Perhaps one of the biggest challenges has been changing the perceptions, and sometimes the systems and procedures, that do not encourage, and sometimes stifle, collaboration. The FIGs program is a true collaboration between academic and student affairs, yet the partners often encounter frustrating and sometimes amusing challenges from institutional structures that do not accommodate such a venture. Because academic and student affairs have their own support structures, various "crossover" issues became challenges. For example, questions arose regarding which letterhead and format to use, what business cards were appropriate and what they should say, who has signing responsibility for the budget, and so on. Though seemingly petty, these issues had to be resolved.

Although the program has encountered some frustrating challenges, we did not experience some challenges we might have anticipated. Faculty involvement was much easier to obtain than expected. In the first year, faculty were identified and recruited with a little effort, but much less than expected. Since then, some faculty have returned year after year and have suggested, nominated, and even recruited some of their peers. Although the program uses some academic administrative and support staff (for example, advisors, program coordinators), over 75 percent of the program cofacilitators are tenured or tenure-track faculty, including many full professors—no small achievement at a research I institution. Compensation also has not been a factor in faculty participation or satisfaction. Faculty cofacilitators receive a $250 stipend for educational expenses (for example, travel, books, subscriptions), but many use these funds to support activities with their FIG students, even though a small pool of money is available for these purposes. Academic departments also have been willing partners in the FIGs program, and even have suggested FIG course combinations.

As the program has expanded, the quality and number of students seeking peer advisor positions have not diminished. In recent years this has been bolstered by the influx of students who participated in FIGs as freshmen and now, as upperclass students, want to provide a similar experience for new students.

How Was the Program Evaluated?

Evaluation of the FIGs program was conducted in four phases, as described below.

Evaluation Process. The first phase of the evaluation focused on student satisfaction and was conducted by the FIGs coordinator. In the second phase, researchers in the student life studies department of the division of student affairs conducted a comprehensive, longitudinal research project to determine the effectiveness of the program. Students' academic records were examined to determine whether participating in the FIGs program was associated with higher levels of academic achievement and persistence than those of students who did not participate.

In the third phase, first-year students were surveyed twice. First, in the fall, students completed the MU Freshman Survey, a locally developed instrument that provided information about the extent to which students were able to fit into the university culture, as well as their commitment to succeeding at

MU. During the winter term, students were surveyed again, this time with the College Student Experiences Questionnaire (CSEQ), which provides measures of the quantity and quality of students' involvement in and out of class, their interactions with faculty and peers, and their efforts to integrate their first-year experiences. The CSEQ also elicited data about students' perceptions of their learning and development at MU. Finally, parents of students participating in the FIGs were surveyed to obtain their perceptions of the impact of the program on their freshman's success.

Evaluation Results. Examination of the academic records of first-time freshmen revealed that students in the FIGs program were significantly more successful than other students, particularly in terms of their retention. Of the 225 students who participated in the FIGs program in fall 1995, all but ten were enrolled for the winter term, a 96 percent retention rate. In comparison, the fall-to-winter retention rate for other students was 91 percent. FIGs participants also had significantly higher one-year retention rates than other students (87 percent versus 81 percent) as well as significantly higher grade point averages, even when controlling for differences in entering ability.

Both the MU Freshman Survey and the CSEQ provided important data about the relationship between the FIGs program and the development of identity, involvement in out-of-class experiences, interaction with faculty and peers, and integration of information gathered from in- and out-of-class experiences. Data from the MU Freshman Survey, for example, revealed that students in the FIGs program reported significantly higher levels of academic integration and institutional commitment than did other students. Three scales from the College Student Experiences Questionnaire provided data about students' involvement during the first year of college, and students in the FIGs program reported significantly higher levels of involvement than other students on all three scales. Furthermore, informal interaction with faculty outside class was higher for the FIGs students on both the MU Freshman Survey and the CSEQ, and the intellectual content of these interactions was significantly greater for FIGs students than other students. Moreover, FIGs students described higher levels of interaction with peers. Participation in the FIGs program also provided more opportunities for students to integrate in- and out-of-class experiences; FIGs participants reported significantly higher levels of integration of course information than did other students.

Some of the most important findings of the fall and winter surveys were related to learning and development during students' first year at MU. FIGs students who responded to the MU Freshman Survey and the CSEQ reported significantly greater gains in communication skills and general education than did other students.

Evaluations regarding student satisfaction revealed that 85 percent of FIGs participants would recommend the program to a friend, and an additional 6 percent would recommend the program with minor modifications. Out-of-state students and students of color expressed particularly high levels of satisfaction with the program. Furthermore, survey results obtained from parents were uniformly positive and they often described the "transformational" impact of the program on their freshmen.

Recommendations and Implications

We offer the following recommendations for persons at institutions seeking to establish collaborative partnerships between academic affairs and student affairs, including programs similar to FIGs:

1. Identify critical issues. Academic and student affairs leaders, along with key stakeholders, should ascertain common issues or problems, the solutions for which require collaboration. Student affairs staff also should take an active role in helping academic departments achieve their goals and objectives.

2. Identify partners and allies. Once common issues are identified, look for partners who have a commitment to address the issues, an understanding of relevant campus operations, and the authority to institute and support changes. Consider forming both a large stakeholders group that will establish general concepts and issues and a small core group that can manage operational details and work effectively. Be sure that both groups maintain a balance between student and academic affairs membership. Both also should include students as well as persons with expertise in assessment.

3. Locate existing models. Are there programs at other institutions or best practices on which a new initiative can be based? At Missouri, the FIGs program was modeled after successful programs at the Universities of Oregon and Washington.

The next set of recommendations is offered for faculty and staff interested in launching a FIG program:

1. Establish a timeline. Begin the project in a measured and deliberate fashion. Compile and overlap all calendars and schedules for relevant departments and processes, including admissions and recruitment, advising, registration, orientation, printing and publication, residence hall contracting and assignment, and so forth. Identify the key components and steps necessary for the program. Develop a "backward-planning" schedule for all major tasks (that is, establish deadlines and work backward, setting earlier deadlines for each preliminary step).

2. Identify appropriate courses and themes. Examine current majors, particularly those in high demand or that are particularly challenging, to determine which might be well suited to FIGs. Use existing courses to avoid the challenges associated with developing new ones. Look for courses offered in multiple sections or which coincide with institutional requirements (for example, general education or core curriculum courses). Select faculty who use effective teaching methods, including frequent opportunities for feedback.

3. Develop a pro-seminar. Adapt successful classes on freshman year experience that focus on topics essential for effective transition and first-year student success; for example, registration, computing skills (e-mail, Internet

research), time management, use of the library, location of campus resources, and communication with faculty and peers. Each pro-seminar curriculum should offer some elements consistent to all FIGs and others that can be designed through collaboration between the peer advisor and faculty. Whenever possible, discussions, assignments, or field trips and visiting speakers should be relevant to the FIG theme and allow for integration of class work with out-of-class experiences. Strongly consider holding the pro-seminar in residence hall spaces.

4. Create shared living arrangements. Identify halls or residence hall floors that currently have moderate to low retention to avoid displacing current residents. FIG materials should indicate which FIGs are assigned to which residence halls. If possible, avoid forcing difficult choices by permitting mutual roommate requests and FIG participation. Assign FIG students prior to placing other students. FIG students should be assigned in as close proximity as possible if they cannot be assigned to the same floor. Combine FIGs with living and learning communities of similar themes (for example, science or engineering) to strengthen those communities, or in a location where new learning communities are planned.

5. Recruit faculty partners. Selectively and actively recruit faculty who are tenured or full professors (who might not face as strenuous demands for research and publication as pretenure faculty), those with college-aged children, those who have won teaching awards, and those with strong credibility with their colleagues. Ideally, a cofacilitator will be one of the faculty members teaching one of the three courses in which students are coenrolled, or within the same department. Work with department chairs to solicit support and to recognize contributions of faculty. If necessary, use academic support staff (advisors, program coordinators, and tutors) as facilitators.

6. Identify student staff. Determine whether student staff positions will be new or adaptations of existing positions. Recruit students with strong academic abilities and interpersonal skills; solicit nominations from faculty. Evaluate candidates' presentation and teaching abilities in the selection process. Strive to coordinate the student staff members' majors with the theme of their FIG assignment. Integrate training of peer advisors with that of other residence life paraprofessionals.

7. Provide FIG orientation. Use elements of, and integrate with, existing orientation programs, but also include aspects specifically for FIGs. This will include an introduction and opportunity for informal interaction with faculty and staff through team building or experiential education initiatives. A reading project, sent to students prior to their arrival or distributed to students at orientation, followed by focused discussions will reinforce the academic focus of the FIGs program. An orientation program before the start of classes should include information about where the shared courses will be held, location of academic resources, and a visit to the bookstore to identify required textbooks. Preliminary computer training, especially e-mail and access to the computing mainframe, would be particularly helpful.

8. Develop strategies to implement the FIGs program. Prepare admissions, faculty, advisors, and support staff with a series of information sessions. Coordinate the FIGs application with housing application and other mailings. Set the FIGs application deadline prior to the housing contract and assignment deadline. Assign students to FIGs first, then assign them to housing. Allow students with advance placement or college credit to participate, by either assigning them to a higher level course in the same discipline or allowing them to coenroll in two courses. Notify students of their FIG assignment prior to summer registration or orientation, and continue to allow students to fill vacant space as long as possible. Have peer advisors contact students over the summer, prior to their arrival.

9. Conduct assessments. Establish assessment criteria prior to initiating the program, but strongly consider using grade point average, retention, satisfaction, and general education outcomes. Use both qualitative and quantitative assessment techniques. Institute a longitudinal study, tracking participants throughout their college careers. Include faculty and parents in the assessment, not only to solicit their perceptions, but also to inform them about and promote investment in the program. Share results widely with faculty, staff, and key decision makers.

Conclusion

Developing successful partnerships, such as the one described in this chapter, requires leadership, collaboration, compromise, risk-taking, and a fundamental examination of prevailing educational assumptions. Partnerships also require hard work, tenacity, and perseverance if they are to be nurtured and sustained. When appropriately implemented, however, there are many important benefits for the partners and their institution.

In the process of implementing the FIG program at MU, we realized that by encouraging change and promoting cooperation, we might receive a host of unexpected benefits. Indeed, a program as ambitious as FIGs only works if the university "early registers" students in a number of classes at the same time it assigns them to blocks of housing. Early registration has its own advantages: It allows departments to respond to a variety of enrollment pressures, it allows the university a competitive advantage in converting prospective students to enrolled students, and it allows advisors the opportunity to place advisees into a number of courses while spaces are still available.

Furthermore, as much as a program such as FIGs is intended to affect success of freshmen, an unintended result is its effect on upperclassmen who serve as peer advisors. In turn, their role as PAs allows them, as undergraduates, to serve in quasi-teaching roles by allowing them to strengthen their own success in their chosen field by teaching their subject matter to others. Finally, and perhaps most interesting, a program intended to promote the success of freshmen has the corollary benefit of allowing faculty to participate in the improvement of undergraduate education without requiring more of them than their status at a research I institution might warrant.

The preceding unintended benefits, when coupled with the successful achievement of various intended outcomes, supports the efficacy of creating powerful partnerships that connect the two divisions on campus most committed to student success: academic affairs and student affairs. The results of such partnerships not only reinvigorate undergraduate education, but they are also equally, and profoundly, invigorating for all parties involved.

CHARLES C. SCHROEDER is vice chancellor for student affairs at the University of Missouri–Columbia.

FRANKIE D. MINOR is director of residential life at the University of Missouri–Columbia.

THEODORE A. TARKOW is associate dean, College of Arts and Sciences, at the University of Missouri–Columbia.

This chapter outlines practical considerations in developing cross-campus partnerships that support connections between in- and out-of-class experiences.

Partnerships to Connect In- and Out-of-Class Experiences

Sarah B. Westfall

American colleges and universities traditionally have offered students rich experiences both in and out of the classroom. Often the in-class and out-of-class lives of students have competed with one another, at least in the eyes of faculty and administrators (Brubacher and Rudy, 1997). The mutually reinforcing nature of these experiences was a hallmark of early American colleges and, happily, is being rediscovered and redefined as we conclude the twentieth century. Indiana University Bloomington (IUB) provides one illustration of how in- and out-of-class experiences can be combined at a large research institution. This chapter outlines practical considerations in developing cross-campus partnerships that support connections between in- and out-of-class experiences. A variety of cross-campus efforts are described, but the Freshman Interest Groups (FIGs) program at Indiana is used as a case in point. Although the University of Missouri FIGs program described in the previous chapter by Schroeder, Minor, and Tarkow served as a model for the development of FIGs at IUB, the differences in the nature of partnerships and collaboration at the two institutions—and the implications of those differences for the FIG programs—are informative.

Background and Context

Several aspects of IUB facilitated the recent development of both FIGs and other partnerships to support student learning. First, the notion of connecting in- and out-of-class experiences at IUB was not new. Programs intended to help students bridge what might otherwise be a gap between academic and nonacademic aspects of their lives had been in operation for many years. For example, the Collins Living Learning Center, a residence hall offering experimental academic programs administered by the College of Arts and Sciences, has thrived for more than two decades. In addition, courses, academic advising, and thematic communities with ties to academic departments (language houses, for example) have been available in IUB residence halls for over fifteen years. The relationships resulting from these efforts contribute to an overall campus ethos of collaboration and cooperation. This is a particularly important factor in supporting new cross-campus collaborations: We have had success in the past, we already have developed effective cross-campus relationships, and we are able to build on both the successes and our relationships.

A second important element was having the right people and structures in the right places at the right time. During the past five years, several personnel and organizational changes occurred that supported and facilitated efforts to combine in- and out-of-class experiences. Among these changes were (1) a new university president, (2) the creation of an enrollment services division, with leadership at the vice-chancellor level, (3) reorganization of the university division (academic home to over 95 percent of freshmen, 50 percent of sophomores, and 44 percent of all undergraduates), (4) reorganization of the Division of Residential Programs and Services, and (5) the appointment of campus experts on student learning to posts in academic affairs. These changes aligned resources with a commitment to improve undergraduate education as they created administrative priorities and structures that accommodated and expanded cross-campus collaboration. In short, the organizational changes fully supported campus-wide collaboration.

A third factor supporting collaboration at IUB was a grant to support institutional efforts to increase graduation rates. The grant, funded by the Lilly Endowment, provided an incentive to expand and initiate programs to increase student persistence to graduation. The advantages of this grant cannot be overstated. Since student persistence is influenced by multiple institutional factors, the grant requires collaboration among many institutional entities. At IUB, the grant has capitalized on extant collaborative relationships by drawing new attention to long-standing collaborative programs, and it has provided funds to launch new programs. Also, external funding helps ensure that no single department bears the full financial burden of implementing new programs to improve student persistence to graduation.

Finally, a widely shared belief that IUB should enhance the experience of first-year students has led to a collective focus on freshmen. Recent criticism of undergraduate education at large research universities (Boyer Commission on Educating Undergraduates in the Research University, 1998) coincided with a campus-based priority of improving undergraduate education. Though undergraduate education is a broad topic with a number of potential starting points, the freshman year is especially important. By helping students be more successful right from the start—giving realistic messages about academic expectations, redesigning large freshman courses, and providing academic support services where students live, to name three examples—we believe that the whole undergraduate experience will be strengthened.

Although other contextual factors are important, prior relationships, key personnel and organizational changes, grant support, and an early interest in the freshman experience are essential to the story of efforts to connect and combine in- and out-of-class experiences, including Freshman Interest Groups at Indiana University.

Freshman Interest Groups

In late October 1997, Freshman Interest Groups (FIGs) officially began at Indiana University Bloomington. During the summer of 1997, the university received a grant from the Lilly Endowment to increase the number of students who graduate from the university. Freshman Interest Groups were proposed as one of eleven initiatives to fulfill the intent of the grant. FIGs can improve retention of first-year students, thereby contributing, eventually, to an increased graduation rate.

FIGs provide one model of learning communities. Learning communities are curricular structures that provide students the opportunity to more deeply understand and integrate their learning through greater intellectual and social coherence and engagement (Gabelnick, MacGregor, Matthews, and Smith, 1990). That is, learning communities provide curricular and environmental experiences that enhance students' ability to connect strongly to the university, both academically and socially. Intentional and substantive interaction with peers and instructors is often a hallmark of learning communities. FIGs are especially well suited to large campuses and are conceptually easy to understand; students sharing a common academic and social frame of reference in a small community are more likely to feel connected to the institution and are more likely to succeed. FIGs use existing courses, residential arrangements, and administrative processes, so it is a relatively low-cost program to initiate.

The success of FIG programs at IUB's sister institutions, especially the model at the University of Missouri–Columbia, made such a program attractive to Indiana. FIG students demonstrated better student learning and performance, better social integration, and stronger institutional commitment and retention rates for FIG students than did their non-FIG peers (Minor, 1997). Although all of the results from Missouri were appealing, the potential benefit to student retention was an ideal match with the goal of the Lilly Endowment grant. Retention improvement attributed to FIGs at Missouri strongly supported the overall IUB grant goal of increasing the number of graduates from the university.

Based largely on the model at Missouri, FIGs at Indiana include residential and curricular components. A FIG is a group of up to twenty-three first-year students who live near each other in the residence halls and who, typically, coenroll in four courses. Of the four courses, three are courses that help students fulfill distribution requirements or begin work in a major area. The fourth course is a one-credit pass-fail FIG Seminar. This seminar is taught by a peer instructor, an accomplished junior or senior also living in residence, who has completed over thirty hours of training. The FIG Seminar focuses on helping students make the academic transition to university-level work and on acquainting students with the vast cultural and intellectual resources of the campus. In addition to teaching the FIG Seminar, the peer instructor serves as an academic resource (for referral to academic support services, as an example) as well as a model of academic success at Indiana.

At Indiana, twenty FIGs were planned for fall 1998. In keeping with the requirements of the Lilly grant, that number will increase by ten each year until a total of fifty FIGs is offered. Having fifty FIGs will allow approximately one-sixth of the freshman class to participate in the program, a number deemed optimal in the grant proposal. Due to the residential and academic nature of FIGs, several important partners are involved in implementing the program: residential programs and services, academic advising, the registrar's office, and more than two dozen individual academic departments and schools. Less prominent (that is, offices with relatively less direct responsibility for components of the FIG program) partners include admissions, orientation programs, the undergraduate library, publications, institutional research, and instructional support services. Absent any of these partners, the FIG program, as one effort to combine in- and out-of-class experiences and hence improve student retention at Indiana, would never have happened. Because FIGs have implications for multiple functional areas, the cooperation of each partner is integral to the success of the program.

Effective Partnerships

Combining students' in- and out-of-class experiences, as the FIG program does, requires healthy campus partnerships. If these efforts are to succeed, academic affairs and student affairs professionals must become familiar, valued collaborators. Though these partnerships have many complexions, the common feature is a genuine understanding that each area has much to offer and gain from the other.

In addition to the FIG program at Indiana, a variety of new and developing efforts involving academic affairs, student affairs, and others are under way. One example is a concerted effort to change the nature of Indiana's summer orientation program so that it is more academically purposeful. Specifically, we are sending clearer messages about expectations for university-level academic work, about the central role of academics at Indiana, and about the range of academic resources and programs available to students. This has required the cooperation of every major academic unit on campus as well as admissions, advising, residential programs and services, student activities, and academic support services. Efforts to integrate career development into major programs of study are on the docket, as is the development of an academic "early-warning system" involving the registrar's office, academic advisors, and residential life staff. The department of residential programs and services has relinquished space in two residence halls so that academic support centers with full tutoring and support services are available to residents during the evening hours. Thematic communities, residential programs that enable students to live together and pursue common interests (academic, artistic, cultural, and social), are growing and continue to benefit from faculty participation. A final example is the Intensive Freshman Seminar, which enables first-year students to come to campus three weeks early in the summer to complete a three-credit course with a small cohort of other new students. This requires collaboration with admissions, residential life, the registrar's office, and a variety of academic departments.

One of the most helpful and unusual partnerships at Indiana is the "Frosh_Up" group. Started by two colleagues after a lunch during which they discussed issues related to the freshman year, Frosh_Up is a fluid group of faculty members and administrators from all parts of campus. It is an informal group with no formal charge or task and changing membership, but it includes people from all levels of the university who have an interest in and responsibility for freshman students. The most important purpose it serves is communication about campus and freshman issues, but it also provides an informal means to develop relationships that support collaborative efforts. The stronger academic emphasis of summer orientation, for example, was supported and discussed at length by the Frosh_Up group.

How do healthy campus partnerships develop? As mentioned earlier, Indiana has a history of collaborative work. In addition, support from the highest levels of the university is important, as is a shared vision that combining in- and out-of-class experiences is beneficial to students and to the academic program. This vision, especially as it supports the academic program and student success, is widely shared at IUB. One of the reasons the vision is widely shared is that institutional leaders are informed and vocal about the benefits. Building on existing professional relationships also is a key factor. Familiar and trusted colleagues make excellent collaborative partners.

For FIGs specifically, legwork in developing relationships with partners around campus is central. Nothing can replace personal, face-to-face contact. FIGs do not require an extraordinary effort by any single department or office, but it does require substantial coordination of dozens of efforts. Since FIGs is a brand-new effort, a certain amount of "cold calling" was necessary. This was eased considerably by the presence of a shared and developing vision that collaboration is valued. The profile and publicity given FIGs by the grant award also paved the way for many of these personal contacts—colleagues across campus had heard of FIGs and were interested in learning more.

The appointment of an advisory board comprising representatives from offices as diverse as the undergraduate library, the registrar's office, a campus trio program, residential programs and services, and academic advising has helped cement major partnerships. At IUB, the FIGs Advisory Board is a "thinking group." The sole charge to the group is to help the director think through every conceivable aspect of the program. This helps all of us see the same "big picture" as well as the fine details unique to individual offices. As with the Frosh_Up group, communication is one of the critical functions of an advisory board. Such a body is essential to many collaborative efforts, especially wholly new ones, because they require so much communication and interaction. Politically, an advisory group cultivates support and commitment (the proverbial buy in) that is priceless.

Another factor that has helped develop FIG-related partnerships at Indiana is the adoption of a no-threat approach to garnering cooperation. We made an effort to ensure, as much as possible, that no important partners perceived the program as a threat to their work or priorities. We made every effort to fold the program into existing processes and practices (working with established class schedule timelines, for example), and centralized much of the administrative work in the FIGs office. Even so, an enormous amount of work was done by partners who share a real belief in the benefits of the program. This shared belief is probably the single most important factor in the development of partnerships. If potential partners agree and believe in a program, the partnerships will develop.

Finally, effective communication is crucial. Timely communication, aided greatly at Indiana by electronic mail, is extraordinarily helpful to partners. Part of the no-threat approach of the FIGs program is a commitment to keep partners as informed as possible so they know what is expected of them and what to expect of others. Communication builds trust, the cornerstone of a good partnership.

Challenges in Creating Effective Partnerships

As with any undertaking, there are several obstacles to combining in- and out-of-class experiences and developing the partnerships that support them. Identifying support and resistance, strategy, timing, seeing the terrain, logistics, and learning quickly are the major challenges to developing partnerships.

Identifying Support and Resistance. Finding and fostering support for collaborative campus efforts, and understanding sources and types of resistance, are essential for programs combining in- and out-of-class experiences. One must know who (individuals or departments) is likely to be supportive of collaborative programs and who is not. This generally becomes clear as partnerships and programs take shape, but there are different reasons that some colleagues are supportive and others are not. At IUB, for example, in a responsibility-centered budget milieu, a legitimate concern for many is how participation in a program might affect the budget. If participation in a program risks or requires financial resources that will not be replaced, collaboration is not an attractive option. Another concern is what sort of demand a program makes on a department. If departments perceive that they must change how they operate or take on onerous new tasks, they may not want to become a program partner.

Developing and Maintaining Effective Strategies. Developing and implementing a strategy is an ongoing challenge in creating partnerships and collaborative programs. In the case of the FIGs program at Indiana, grant funding predetermined certain strategic elements. For example, academic departments at IUB can agree to be part of FIGs or not. On other campuses, colleges and schools make the initial commitment to collaborate, and departments are compelled to participate. The grant that funds the FIGs program at IUB, and the general values of the campus, support departmental autonomy in FIG participation. The best strategy for a given campus is consistent with its culture. This will maximize a program's chance of success from planning through implementation.

Addressing Problems of Time and Timing. Determining how much time is necessary to plan collaborative programs and to establish partnerships is difficult. Also, it very well may be the factor over which people implementing a new program have the least control. The time available for thorough planning will often be inadequate and program planners will almost always wish they had more time to think things through. The challenge, therefore, lies in figuring out how much time is needed to most effectively (and feasibly!) do the work of planning and partnership building.

Seeing the Terrain. In collaborative efforts that join offices having widely variant functions and orientations, it is imperative to develop a comprehensive understanding of the effort as a whole. In the same way an aerial photograph shows all of the features of a particular territory, it is important that those involved in collaborative programs "see" as much of the program terrain as possible. Figuring out how to do this is the challenge. Again, in the case of FIGs at IUB, an advisory board comprising individuals from a wide range of offices on campus was the single most helpful and efficient way to see the whole territory. The goal is to see enough of the program terrain to anticipate concerns by potential partners.

Managing Logistics. Coordinating multiple efforts and partnerships requires attention to detail, anticipation, timely communication, and constant clarification. This is also the place where partners will begin to make assessments about the wisdom of the partnership. If basic administrative needs are met, most partners will be pleased. An apt analogy is the role of sanitation work. We may not give lots of thought to it, but we are immediately aware of it if the work is poorly done. The same is true of logistics. They are rarely the central focus in the development of collaborative programs, but they are essential. Logistics are not glamorous, but they are important to partners and to the success of any program. Understanding and attending to all of them is the challenge.

Learning Quickly. The more complex an effort (number of partners, processes to be coordinated, adjustments to "usual" processes, and so on), the more there is to learn. The challenge is getting as much information (historical, logistical, political, to name three categories) as you need as quickly as possible.

Evaluating Collaborative Efforts

Good evaluative information is like gold. It is very valuable, it is surprisingly rare, and there are periodic rushes for it (at budget time, for example). One question everyone involved with collaborative efforts has is, "Did it work?" Evaluation of collaborative efforts must meet the needs of as many partners as possible. The goal of evaluation is to answer the reasonable questions. The best starting place for evaluation is the same starting place for the effort itself—the purpose. Combining in- and out-of-class experiences and developing cross-campus partnerships occurs, at least in part, to fulfill some identified purpose. This purpose must drive the evaluation.

The FIGs program at Indiana University Bloomington is intended to increase student retention, in support of the ultimate goal of increasing the number of students who graduate from the university. Funding for FIGs was granted for this specific purpose, so the fundamental piece of evaluative information needed by the university and the funder is retention data. Are FIG students retained at higher rates than their non-FIG peers are? These data are regularly collected by the registrar and are used to answer the primary question of semester-to-semester and year-to-year retention.

The clarity of purpose for the FIGs program at IUB is one benefit of grant support. Programs that emerge from within an institution, without external funding, may have multiple or fuzzy purposes. This makes evaluation difficult and produces data that are of little use to the campus. A clear purpose may have contributed to collaboration across campus. If so, it will aid evaluation as well.

Beyond the retention purpose of the FIGs program, other information will also be valuable to the university. We collect demographic information from FIGs students to understand how "typical" they are of the general IU student body. We track grade-point averages for FIG students and we also request student satisfaction data from FIG students.

Aside from determining whether a program has fulfilled its purpose, evaluation is the best way to gather formative information that can actually contribute to midstream program improvements. The evaluation plan for FIGs at Indiana was written before the first FIG was ever constructed. The goal of the evaluation program is to provide a loop of information that can be used at any time to improve any facet of the program.

Unintended Consequences of Collaboration

All programs, especially collaborative ones, have unintended consequences. The negative consequences provide opportunities to tune and improve the effort. It is important to attend to these consequences early and effectively to retain the goodwill of partners. The impact of positive unintended consequences is limited only by the creativity of campus colleagues.

One of the most important things to be learned from combining in- and out-of-class experiences in the FIG program at Indiana is the lesson of unintended consequences. Fortunately, most of the unintended consequences have been positive. A good example of this is the preparation of the peer instructors who teach the FIG Seminar. Since Indiana does not have a model of undergraduates teaching and grading each other, we determined that they needed a substantial training program. The training program was intended to prepare the peer instructors fully for their new role. The general framework for training was borrowed from the University of Washington, and the content and approach were tailored for our campus. The unintended consequences of this activity are two-fold. First, the thoroughness of the PI preparation helped develop confidence in the FIG program across campus. Second, the preparation program is being adapted to help train associate instructors (graduate instructors and teaching assistants) on campus. The collaboration that went into developing the PI preparation program not only trained the PIs and established a wonderful working relationship between two offices, it has also borne fruit for the campus beyond the FIG program.

A second unintended consequence of the collaboration behind FIGs at Indiana is the genuine pleasure that goes with developing relationships across campus. It is informative and stimulating to work with partners from different divisions and departments, but (perhaps more important) it is also a lot of fun. The gulf between various offices and departments on campus is not as great as we might believe. The friendly relationships stemming from collaboration have been a delightful, unintended consequence here at Indiana.

Recommendations

Surely anyone involved in combining in- and out-of-class experiences will have recommendations for colleagues with similar interests. The following recommendations are born of the FIGs program at Indiana. Some echo previous parts of the chapter and all are applicable to a wide range of collaborative efforts.

1. Be knowledgeable and articulate about the benefits of combining in- and out-of-class experiences. Share information, research findings, and articles with colleagues, especially potential partners in collaborative efforts. Specific attention to the benefits of collaboration for the academic program and student success can be particularly compelling to colleagues and potential partners. All new programs require advocacy and evidence of success, for the rightness of an idea is unlikely to be persuasive to reluctant collaborators. Garner support from the highest levels possible. The commitment of senior administrators in academic affairs, campus life, residential programs and services, and enrollment services has been indispensable to FIGs at Indiana. Without such support, collaborative efforts are doomed.

2. Build on existing success and relationships. This makes new ideas more familiar and builds confidence. Be clear about how new ideas and partnerships are similar to and different from current ones.

3. Talk with colleagues engaged in similar work at sister institutions. This helps identify potential land mines, provides practical examples of success, and broadens the range of realistic options open to your campus. Secure and allow adequate time for planning. Building support, understanding the complexities of collaborative efforts, and planning for a useful evaluation process all take time. Planning time is an investment in the success of the effort.

4. Understand, as clearly as possible, the concerns of potential partners. Take time to talk with key people individually, offer to talk with groups, and actively ask, "What concerns do you have?" Most important, use this information to prevent problems later on.

5. Articulate potential benefits to partners. Answer the question of what participation will do for individual colleagues, offices, departments, students, and the institution. Also be prepared to talk honestly about the risks or uncertainties of participation. Candor is refreshing and signals realistic expectations.

6. Plan evaluation from the beginning with plenty of input by interested parties and partners. Focus on the purpose and desired outcomes of the program when writing the evaluation plan.

7. Appoint or work with a cross-campus advisory group. This centralizes a range of important people, information, and perspective. Structure the group carefully—an advisory group is different from a task or decision-making group, both of which are more time-consuming than an advisory group.

8. Look for partners in unlikely places. Less prominent partners may emerge as being very important. The instructional consultants at IUB are not a major partner for making FIGs a "go," but they have the primary role in preparing student staff and, serendipitously, have become a major source of support for the program.

9. Keep good records to ensure that you're smarter the second year than the first. Make notes of problems as they occur and refer to them frequently as you plan for the future. This is the best way to avoid repeating mistakes. Develop patience and a willingness to move forward, even in ignorance. New efforts and partnerships often lack a familiar model or precedent. Patience and persistence are prerequisites for program development.

Conclusion

Many colleges and universities in the United States have a distinguished history of strongly demarcating the line between in- and out-of-class experiences for students. Combining these experiences is a new and delicate undertaking for many campuses. At Indiana University Bloomington, the Freshman Interest Groups program is one feasible and effective way to blend in- and out-of-class experiences for first-year students. The benefits of collaborative work across campus are enormous for student success and for the institution as a whole. By understanding institutional context and background, borrowing and developing good models, cultivating cross-campus partnerships, identifying challenges and obstacles, and enlisting the help of colleagues engaged in the same work, efforts to combine in- and out-of-class experiences can be wildly successful. As is true in many cases, what is good for students is good for us and for our institutions as well.

References

Boyer Commission on Educating Undergraduates in the Research University. *Reinventing Undergraduate Education: A Blueprint for America's Research Universities.* New York: Carnegie Foundation for the Advancement of Teaching, 1998.

Brubacher, J. S., and Rudy, W. *Higher Education in Transition: A History of American Colleges and Universities* (4th ed.). New Brunswick, N.J.: Transaction Publishers, 1997.

Gabelnick, F., MacGregor, J., Matthews, R. S., and Smith, B. L. *Learning Communities: Creating Connections Among Students, Faculty, and Disciplines.* New Directions for Teaching and Learning, no. 41. San Francisco: Jossey-Bass, 1990.

Minor, F. D. "Bringing It Home: Integrating Classroom and Residential Experiences." *About Campus,* 1997, 21–22.

SARAH B. WESTFALL is director of the Freshman Interest Groups program and adjunct assistant professor of higher education at Indiana University.

This case study focuses on the Ursuline Studies Program, a collaboration between academic and student affairs at Ursuline College.

The Ursuline Studies Program: A Collaborative Core Curriculum

Martin F. Larréy, Sandra M. Estanek

In 1991, Ursuline College, a small Catholic women's college located in the suburbs of Cleveland, Ohio, implemented a new comprehensive core curriculum that quickly gained national attention because of a feature article in the May 13, 1992, edition of *The New York Times* ("An Ohio College Says Women Learn Differently," 1992). The curriculum was named the Ursuline Studies Program (USP). The Ursuline Studies Program was developed over a three-year period beginning in 1989. It was piloted in 1990 and fully implemented over the next three years. The curriculum had several interesting features. First, the core curriculum was integrated, interdisciplinary, and sequential. Second, the curriculum embodied both learning goals and developmental goals. It was designed to move a student through specific developmental stages and academic competencies. Third, the curriculum modeled a collaborative approach to learning. Its most distinctive feature, however, was its theoretical integrity.

As a college for women, Ursuline College was one of the first institutions of higher education to understand the relevance of the emerging feminist pedagogy of the 1980s. The first three features of the Ursuline Studies curriculum mentioned above were developed in the context of the pioneering work of Belenky, Clinchy, Goldberger, and Tarule in *Women's Ways of Knowing* (1986). The insights of this emerging tradition have come to be understood as relevant to learning per se and not only to the experience of women (Love and Goodsell Love, 1995). The experience of the Ursuline Studies curriculum, too, is thus relevant to higher education in general and not only to women's colleges.

The Ursuline Studies Program remains in place at Ursuline College. It is a successful example of what can be accomplished when a faculty and administration commit themselves to collaborative learning. The curriculum is important to study because it models many of the characteristics now being set forth as necessary to collaborative learning. Love and Goodsell Love (1995) argue that "collaborative learning actively incorporates social and affective dynamics between students and faculty, to enhance intellectual development and learning" (p. 57). They offer several specific strategies for faculty who wish to create a collaborative learning environment. They challenge faculty to "assess social and emotional influences on the learning process and social and emotional outcomes of that process" (p. 67), "incorporate social and emotional elements in the teaching process" (p. 68), "focus on the individual student" (p. 68), and "reflect on your relationship with students and on the role social and emotional elements play in your teaching" (p. 70). Similar principles have been articulated in professional statements such as *The Student Learning Imperative* (American College Personnel Association [ACPA], 1994) and *Powerful Partnerships: A Shared Responsibility for Learning* (American Association for Higher Education [AAHE], American College Personnel Association, and National Association of Student Personnel Administrators [NASPA], 1998). The latter report describes active learning as "a cumulative process involving the whole person, relating past and present, integrating the new with the old, starting from but transcending personal concerns and interests" (AAHE, ACPA, NASPA, 1998, p. 10). Such learning is done by individuals who are socially connected and grounded in particular contexts and experiences.

Collaborative learning has been modeled successfully by the Ursuline Studies Program. Collaboration at Ursuline is practiced on several levels. First, the learning style of the USP classroom is collaborative. Students collaborate with each other in learning projects, and professors act as mentors and facilitators of the learning process, rather than lecturing from the podium. Second, faculty collaborate with each other. The creation of the curriculum was a collaborative effort and many of the USP courses are team-taught. Third, the faculty collaborate with members of the Division of Student Services to address the developmental goals of the curriculum.

The Ursuline Studies core curriculum consists of fourteen courses organized into three developmental stages. Academic and developmental goals were established for each of the three stages. Each stage is anchored by an interdisciplinary course that focuses on the main academic and developmental goals of that particular stage. The first stage is anchored by the Introductory Seminar for traditional aged first-time students and by a similar course called Transitions, which focuses on returning adult students. The second stage is anchored by a course entitled Introduction to Culture, and the third stage is anchored by a capstone Culminating Seminar, which focuses on themes of values and social responsibility. Eleven courses from traditional liberal arts disciplines were redesigned to complement and expand upon the themes of the anchor courses, and these form the content of the USP core curriculum.

The story of the Ursuline Studies Program has been told comprehensively by its first director in *Educating Women at Ursuline College: Curriculum, Collaboration, and Growth* (Carfagna, 1998). Her book focuses on the content and structure of the Ursuline Studies Program, and on the learning outcomes of the curriculum and the assessment of those outcomes. This case study focuses, instead, on the process of creating the curriculum and on aspects of collaboration, particularly the collaboration between the faculty and student services. We will describe, first, the discussions that led to the establishment of the Ursuline Studies Program and to a commitment to collaboration. We then discuss the Introductory Seminar, which has incorporated the most significant collaborative efforts between the faculty and the Division of Student Services.

Both authors were involved in the implementation of the Ursuline Studies Program. The case study is based upon the personal recollections of the authors, minutes and reports of relevant meetings, and conversations with persons involved with the creation and implementation of the core curriculum.

The Ursuline Studies Curriculum: Context

The creation of the Ursuline Studies Program was grounded in three dynamics that came together in the late 1980s: the experience of faculty working with returning nontraditional students; the revision of the College mission statement; and the national conversation about curriculum revision exemplified in the report of the Carnegie Foundation for the Advancement of Teaching, *College: The Undergraduate Experience in America* (Boyer, 1987).

The story of the Ursuline Studies Program actually began in the mid-1970s. The College received an increasing number of inquiries regarding possible matriculation from former students and other women who had interrupted their college experience years earlier to marry and raise a family. Many of these women sought to complete their degrees, some out of a desire for new careers as their children moved into high school and beyond, some out of necessity through divorce and the need to start a new life. The college responded favorably to those requests with a pioneering adult education program. The impact of the incorporation of large numbers of older adult women into the Ursuline student body was expressed in two institutional features: the establishment of a special office for the recruitment and advising of returning adult students and, more relevant for the history of the Ursuline Studies Program, the creation of an introductory seminar parallel to the course required of traditional first-year students.

As many others were to discover, Ursuline found that the outlook, needs, and styles of learning of these women were different from those of traditional age students. Whereas they were apprehensive about their presence in college, they were focused on their educational goals. Most had come to the decision to return to college after personal struggle. They brought significant life experience to their studies, and they wanted to relate their "story" to their new educational experiences. We discovered, however, that the curriculum provided little opportunity for such "story-telling." Two members of the Ursuline community, one a member of the English department, Ann Trivisonno, and the other a counselor in the office of counseling and career services, Marge Diemer, became aware of this and created a team-taught reentry course focused on the needs of returning women.

The course was both creative and improvisational, providing these students with an opportunity to reflect upon their previous experience as well as an opportunity to sharpen their academic skills. The course reintroduced the adult learner to the college experience while also giving her a venue in which she could find her "voice"; in other words, where she could tell her story as a means of restructuring her educational life and providing direction to her aspirations. The course was supported by a grant from the National Endowment for the Humanities. The course perennially had high enrollments and strong evaluations.

The Ursuline Studies Program: Creation

During the mid-1980s, two unrelated assessments emerged. First, the Ursuline faculty was becoming attuned to the currents in higher education, crystallized in the Carnegie report (Boyer, 1987), which called for a more integrated and coherent undergraduate curriculum to replace the distributional model that had emerged in the 1960s. At the same time, the experience of Trivisonno and Diemer in their introductory seminar for adult students demonstrated that an alternative learning experience was possible. This alternative stressed self-disclosure and self-definition, connectedness, collaborative efforts and projects, and the coherence of life and learning.

In the beginning, these two assessments were completely unrelated. Curriculum reform emerged as a priority of the faculty, but they did not yet understand that in terms of generalizing the learning experience of the adult introductory seminar. In 1987, the new vice president for academic affairs held a series of informal consultations with division chairs, department heads, and other faculty leaders, and determined that curriculum reform was an issue to engage. As a consequence of these discussions, the president of the college established a task force of faculty, chaired by the academic vice president, to undertake reform of the core curriculum. It is significant to note that the president recently had led a successful effort to rewrite the college's mission statement. The new mission statement reaffirmed the college as a Catholic college for women, and articulated a holistic approach to education, exemplified in the following sentence: "In all of our services, we strive for the integration of the intellectual, aesthetic, social, psychological, physical, and spiritual dimension of life—the heart of any endeavor to initiate and sustain the search for wisdom" (Ursuline College mission statement, 1987). Reform of the curriculum would take place within the context of this understanding of the mission of Ursuline College.

During 1988–1989, the curriculum task force considered several modifications to the curriculum, but after several months of tinkering with the existing curriculum, they still were not satisfied that they were working toward something credible. Then in the course of one meeting in the spring of 1989, Dr. Trivisonno suggested that perhaps the starting point of the discussion—modifying the existing curriculum—was inhibiting the development of a new perspective and she suggested an alternative. She had read a new book, *Women's*

Ways of Knowing (Belenky, Clinchy, Goldberger, and Tarule, 1986), and what she found there confirmed what she and Ms. Diemer had learned in the course they had developed for adult learners. The book affirmed the experience of learning they pioneered with returning adult women, and it indicated that this experience could be generalized into a comprehensive approach to the curriculum. At the task force's last meeting of 1988–1989 on June 14, 1989, Dr. Trivissono presented a summary of the ideas of *Women's Ways of Knowing.*

When the task force resumed its work in 1989–1990, this new perspective energized and crystallized its work. The decisive step was taken to jettison the old curriculum in its entirety and to begin with blank paper under the guidance of the theoretical framework of *Women's Ways of Knowing.* This theoretical framework posited that the education of women required an approach that was substantially different from what was conventionally practiced in most, if not all, American colleges and universities. Continuous discussion and analyses of *Women's Ways of Knowing* led to a consensus that traditional-aged college women differed only in degree from the returning adult learner; that the psychological structure of women was fundamentally similar and fundamentally different from that of men. On the basis of this perspective, a new type of curriculum could be created.

What were the salient features of this new theoretical structure? First, unlike men, women needed a pedagogical environment in which they could recover and give shape to their "voice"—where their identities could be "reformatted" out of the welter of their previous experience in educational environments that were more competitive and analytical. Second, the methodology of the new curriculum had to stress collaborative and connected learning. Learning had to be interactive, a joint effort of various voices, integrating experience and knowledge into a collaborative whole. Third, this entire process was a series of unfolding stages. One could not form an integrated value system until one had experienced alternative perspectives, but one could not do that if one did not have a sturdy self-identity, but that was not possible if one had not recovered one's "voice." The failure of the old curriculum was that it served up a jumble of discrete pieces of information unrelated to each other and mismatched to the stage of individual educational development. That is why it could not be reformed and why it had to be entirely discarded.

During the fall semester of 1989, the task force delved into the stages of development described in *Women's Ways of Knowing* and began to rethink specific courses and structures in light of that context. The task force proposed a new core curriculum organized into three developmental stages, each anchored by a year-long, team-taught required course. Developmental goals and academic competencies were established for each of the levels. Assessment strategies were proposed. A grant proposal to the Lilly Endowment was written and submitted in December 1989. This grant ultimately was accepted, and Lilly support was received for the development of the core curriculum and the necessary faculty development. In January 1990, a model of this new core curriculum was presented for discussion at a faculty workshop.

This comprehensive institutional effort continued in the spring semester, 1990. After approval by the faculty, the new curriculum was presented to the president for formal acceptance and a budget was developed. This was crucial because the new curriculum was more labor intensive than the older one and thus more expensive. It was decided that the new curriculum would be phased in over a three-year period, that the Introductory Seminar for all new students would be piloted in 1990–1991. Faculty interested in teaching the pilot were selected and began work on the master syllabus for that course.

The new curriculum also required a change in the administrative structure of the academic area to signal the value that the college community placed upon it. Ursuline Studies was created as an academic division on par with the other divisions. An elected Ursuline Studies Committee was established, and by the end of the year the first director of the Ursuline Studies Program, Sr. Rosemarie Carfagna, was appointed.

To this point, the new core curriculum was a project of the faculty with the support of the executive leadership of the college. Student services staff were not included formally in the discussions that led to the new curriculum, even though the minutes indicate that it was presumed that the new Introductory Seminar would include a cocurricular component with which the Student Services area would be involved in some way. It is significant to note that it was the President's Council and not the faculty that added a representative of the Division of Student Services, appointed by the vice president for student services, to the new Ursuline Studies Committee.

The Introductory Seminar: Formal Collaboration Between Faculty and Student Affairs

The first phase of the Ursuline Studies curriculum to be fully implemented was the Introductory Seminar for all new students. That year-long course involved the closest collaboration between the teaching faculty and the Division of Student Services. It was through the experience of that course that the formal structural connection between the two areas was forged. A pilot test of the Introductory Seminar occurred in 1990–1991 and the seminar was fully implemented for all new students in 1991–1992.

The primary purpose of the seminar was to help students move from a position of received knowing to one of subjective knowing (Belenky and others, 1986). That is, seminar experiences were designed to facilitate development of "a perspective from which truth and knowledge are conceived of as personal, private, and subjectively known or intuited" (Belenky and others, 1986, p. 15), in contrast to a perspective in which sources of knowledge and truth are conceived as external to the individual. Although the seminar thus incorporated elements of "writing across the curriculum" and "the freshman experience," it did so in ways unique to the goals of women's development. For example, course designers assumed that if a student writes about her own experience, or about new and shared experiences, she can learn to write well *and* develop her own voice. In this way, academic and developmental goals can be achieved in the same process.

The course was structured to achieve these goals. It contained elements typical of Freshman Experience courses, such as credit for participation in cocurricular activities, introduction to college services and personnel, and discussion of values and issues developmentally appropriate to first-year students. Through journaling, reflective essays, and the reading of novels such as *I Know Why the Caged Bird Sings* (Angelou, 1969) these experiential elements were connected to the learning process. The master syllabus for the course was developed collaboratively by the faculty who agreed to participate in the pilot project in 1990–1991. Since 1990, different faculty have taught this course using that master syllabus. Some specific features have changed but the course remains essentially the same at this writing.

The two features of formal collaboration between the faculty and the Division of Student Services that were developed in conjunction with the Introductory Seminar deserve special mention: (1) the wellness requirement of the core curriculum, and (2) the connection between the curriculum and career services. In both of these areas the faculty agreed to delegate formal responsibility for aspects of the core curriculum to members of the Division of Student Services.

The question of what kind of physical education requirement should be part of the new curriculum had been discussed since the creation of the core curriculum task force in 1989. When the Ursuline Studies Committee was established in 1990, a subcommittee was formed to develop a proposal for a new physical education requirement. The subcommittee worked through the fall semester of 1990. Their proposal changed the focus of the physical education curriculum away from a typical activity course to a wellness requirement individually tailored to a diverse population of women. The committee proposed that the wellness requirement be incorporated into the Introductory Seminar, but that a wellness coordinator be hired to develop and manage that part of the curriculum. That person would be a member of the Division of Student Services and would report to the vice president for student services. The proposal was accepted and the first wellness coordinator was hired in 1991. At that point, student services became formally responsible for an aspect of the core curriculum.

A similar pattern was followed in the area of career services. There was, however, less formal discussion than there was about the wellness requirement. The minutes of meetings held in 1989–1991 do not indicate a discussion of the role of career development in the new curriculum as they do the development of the wellness requirement. Career development had been an important aspect of the original introductory course for adult women taught by Trivissono and Diemer. It is possible to assume that incorporating such an aspect into the new core was accepted with little discussion. What did emerge in 1990 was a commitment to include the Myers-Briggs Type Inventory in the requirements of the Introductory Seminar and to hire an additional counselor in the office of counseling and career services to support the requirements of the Ursuline Studies Program. The first USP counselor, as she was known, was hired for the 1991–1992 academic year. Like the wellness coordinator hired in the same period, this person was a member of the Division of Student Services. Both positions continue today and are held by new people. This demonstrates that the formal collaboration that these hires pioneered has continued and is now presumed.

Significance of the Ursuline Studies Program

This chapter has presented a brief descriptive case study of the Ursuline Studies Program at Ursuline College. According to Merriam (1988), "Innovative programs and practices are often the focus of descriptive case studies in education. Such studies often form a database for future comparison and theory building" (p. 27). The Ursuline Studies Program is such an innovative program. The program was created during a two-year period from 1988 to 1990. It was implemented in three phases over the next three years.

It is clear in retrospect that the creation of the Ursuline Studies Program followed the classic model of program development outlined by Moore and Delworth (1976). This model consists of five steps: (1) initiation of the program, (2) the planning process, (3) the pilot project, (4) full implementation, and (5) refinement. Initiation of the program includes conducting a needs assessment, developing an idea for a program that responds to the need, assembling those who will conduct the program, and developing the necessary resources. The planning process includes agreeing upon appropriate goals and developing the structure that will accomplish the goals of the program. It also includes developing a plan for the assessment of the program. The next step is to develop a pilot project and to conduct a formative evaluation. What was learned should be incorporated into the program, which is then launched on a full-scale level and refined even further.

Although it is true that the planning and implementation of the Ursuline Studies core curriculum followed these steps, the problem with characterizing the process in these terms is that it minimizes its fluid and open-ended nature. The faculty who met to revise the core curriculum did not have the vision of the Ursuline Studies Program in their minds when they began their work. They met initially, as many faculties were doing, to modify the curriculum to make it more effective. In the course of their discussions, they came to the collective conclusion that a new framework was needed to accomplish their goal. *Women's Ways of Knowing* helped them restructure their discussions in terms of a new theoretical model. Their discussions led them in directions they had not initially imagined and opened up new possibilities. An example of this is the collaboration with student services and the formal delegation of two aspects of the core curriculum to the Division of Student Services. This collaboration emerged because it made sense as the program developed, not because there was any commitment to such collaboration in advance.

As with all case studies, many of the dynamics described here are specific to the situation of Ursuline College as a private, women's college; however, several themes can be identified in this case that are relevant to any college or university that chooses to embark on a process of collaboration and innovation.

1. The importance of theory: As has been stated, the developmental framework in *Women's Ways of Knowing* helped the curriculum revision task force reinforce the validity of the experience of the faculty who had worked with nontraditional students, and also helped them develop new structures to accomplish their educational goals. One of these new structures was the collaboration with student services. Essentially, the faculty became committed to a vision of education that was holistic and collaborative. Collaboration with the Division of Student Services emerged naturally from this new vision and was necessary to its realization. As this case study indicated, that formal collaboration was not part of the initial planning; however, it is now an integral part of the Ursuline Studies Program. It is thus surprising to discover that it was not part of the initial discussion. One of the participants in the task force who shared her archival material wrote in an e-mail, "I also found it interesting that there was no real discussion of student services even though it is an integral part of the core! I thought, for sure, there would have been something in the minutes." Rather than causing concern, this should illustrate the power of theory to take practitioners in new directions.

2. The importance of mission: The Ursuline Studies curriculum succeeded because it was consistent with the mission of Ursuline College. This is a particularly important lesson for private colleges whose resources are often limited. These institutions must have the discipline to program from mission, not need (Larréy, 1998). In other words, small schools with limited resources cannot do everything, but they can prioritize their resources to do some important things exceptionally well because of their very smallness. Ursuline Studies is a good example of this. Designing an integrative core curriculum that incorporated the insights of the emerging feminist pedagogy was consistent with the mission of the college as a women's college, therefore it was possible to garner the support and resources it needed to become an institutional priority. However, because the college was small, it could aspire to provide this opportunity to all students, not only to a select group of students in a special program.

3. The importance of leadership: Because of this very need to prioritize resources—saying yes to some projects and therefore needing to say no to others—leadership is particularly important to ambitious and innovative projects such as the Ursuline Studies Program. This was true of Ursuline Studies both within the faculty itself and across the institution. This new curriculum required significant resources. It also required faculty to commit themselves to new teaching methods and to new relationships. The program succeeded because champions emerged among the senior faculty and the executive leadership of the institution. Again, the fact that the new curriculum was clearly

grounded in the mission of the institution facilitated the emergence of these champions.

Leadership also has been important to the success of the program over time. The program has not been without its stresses. Tension has always existed between the need for the theoretical integrity of the curriculum and the need for flexibility. There always has been a tension between the academic goals and the developmental goals of the curriculum and how much time should be devoted to each. These stresses are built into the nature of the program. They are overcome through the willingness of the leadership to engage them honestly.

4. The importance of structure: These stresses also have been overcome because Ursuline Studies is now part of the fundamental structure of the college. The curriculum is now ten years old. Many of the original visionaries have retired, returned to their academic departments, or left the college for new challenges and opportunities. The two student services positions related to the curriculum are now held by new people. The curriculum is soon to be under the leadership of its third director. The vision has survived into this next generation because it is now structured into the institution.

As this chapter demonstrates, all four features described above were essential for the project to succeed because each was an aspect whose omission would have jeopardized any opportunity for permanence. Although certain characteristics of the Ursuline Studies Program are clearly related to the specific character of the college from which it emanated, we believe that this description of its development and establishment clearly shows that similar undertakings may confidently be considered at other, and even different, types of institutions. We also believe that as the topic of collaborative efforts between academic affairs and student affairs appears more prominently and frequently on agendas related to higher education, a study of the Ursuline Studies Program would be instructive to those seeking models concerning this timely subject.

References

American Association for Higher Education, American College Personnel Association, and National Association of Student Personnel Administrators (Joint Task Force). *Powerful Partnerships: A Shared Responsibility for Learning.* Washington, D.C.: American Association for Higher Education, American College Personnel Association, and National Association of Student Personnel Administrators, 1998.

American College Personnel Association. *The Student Learning Imperative.* Washington, D.C.: American College Personnel Association, 1994.

Angelou, M. *I Know Why the Caged Bird Sings.* New York: Random House, 1969.

"An Ohio College Says Women Learn Differently, So It Teaches That Way." *The New York Times,* May 13, 1992, p. B7.

Belenky, M. F., Clinchy, B. M., Goldberger, N. R ., and Tarule, J. M. *Women's Ways of Knowing: The Development of Self, Voice, and Mind.* New York: Basic, 1986.

Boyer, E. L. *College: The Undergraduate Experience in America*. New York: Harper and Row, 1987.

Carfagna, R. *Educating Women at Ursuline College: Curriculum, Collaboration, and Growth*. Lewiston, N.Y.: Mellen Press, 1998.

Larréy, M. F. "Clouded Horizons: Catholic Higher Education in the Coming Decade." *Catholic Education: A Journal of Inquiry and Practice*, 1998, 1 (4), 414–426.

Love, P. G., and Goodsell Love, A. *Enhancing Student Learning: Intellectual, Social, and Emotional Integration*. Washington, D.C.: The George Washington University, Graduate School of Education and Human Development, 1995. (ASHE-ERIC Higher Education Report No. 4.)

Merriam, S. B. *Case Study Research in Education: A Qualitative Approach*. San Francisco: Jossey-Bass, 1988.

Moore, M., and Delworth, U. *Training Manual for Student Service Program Development*. Boulder, Colo.: Western Interstate Commission for Higher Education, 1976.

MARTIN F. LARRÉY is vice president for academic affairs at the University of St. Francis in Joliet, Illinois.

SANDRA M. ESTANEK is vice president for student development at Alvernia College in Reading, Pennsylvania.

One way to facilitate greater collaboration is merging student affairs into academic affairs. Such mergers create opportunities and challenges for everyone involved.

Merging with Academic Affairs: A Promotion or Demotion for Student Affairs?

Jerry Price

The previous chapters in this sourcebook have noted and illustrated the value of student affairs and academic affairs partnerships in enhancing student learning. Much of this value is grounded in the recognition that student learning does not stop at the classroom walls, but "takes place informally and incidentally, beyond explicit teaching or the classroom in casual contacts with faculty and staff, peers, campus life, active social and community involvements, and unplanned but fertile and complex situations" (Joint Task Force on Student Learning, 1998). The Kellogg Commission on the Future of State and Land Grant Universities (1997) stated that in the learning community of the future the college experience will "integrate the 'hidden curriculum,' including cocurricular experiences, much more directly into the learning experience" (Kellogg Commission, 1997, p. 22).

Yet another reason academic affairs and student affairs partnerships are valuable is the complementary strengths and weaknesses faculty and student affairs professionals bring to campus learning environments. Together, academic affairs and student affairs can bring "integration and coherence to a traditionally fragmented, compartmentalized, and often random approach to achieving important undergraduate education outcomes" (Schroeder, 1996, p. 2). Student affairs staff traditionally are considered experts on who students are, whereas faculty are regarded as experts on what and how students learn; the gaps in one group's strength are filled by the strengths of the other.

Cross (1996) used a vision analogy to illustrate this point: Student affairs professionals tend to see the world of higher education through bifocals, through which their focus constantly alternates between individual students and the larger student community; these frequent changes of view can lead to a "blurry area where the two fields of vision unite" (p. 5). Faculty, on the other hand, tend to suffer from tunnel vision, in which they usually have "excellent focus on student learning for the fifty-minute class period, but they don't see the student's twenty-four-hour day filled with course work, study, hasty meals, personal relationships, health concerns, financial problems, insecurities, and uncertainties, all of which affect classroom learning but also produce other learning that seems peripheral to the lives of discipline-oriented faculty" (Cross, 1996, p. 5). Together, their contributions to student learning more than make up for their short-comings.

One way some institutions are attempting to capitalize on these complementary strengths and facilitate greater collaboration is by merging student affairs staff and responsibilities into the division of academic affairs. The purpose of this chapter is to describe and examine the issues to consider when contemplating, or experiencing, such a merger.

Merging Student Affairs With Academic Affairs

In most cases, a merger of academic and student affairs results in changes in reporting relationships; typically, the senior student affairs officer reports to the senior academic officer, not the president, and becomes a member of the senior academic officer's leadership team. This new structure can encourage greater interaction among faculty, academic administrators, and student affairs professionals; as a result, it can be a catalyst for developing effective partnerships on a variety of worthwhile learning ventures, such as teaching, research, curriculum development, and creation of learning communities.

Although the specific objectives for a merger may differ according to the needs and characteristics of each institution, it is important that the motivation for the merger be grounded in the desire to enhance student learning. A merger that is initiated primarily by a desire for budget savings—although it may accomplish short-term budget objectives—is almost certain to fail to enhance student learning. Instead, the merger should begin with the shared desire to make the student affairs mission and the academic affairs mission integrated components of one comprehensive, institutional learning environment. In addition to having objectives grounded in student learning goals, it is important to have a consensus on what those specific goals are. "Vision is not about buying in but about accessing the individual and collective sense of what matters most" (Brown, 1997, p. 7). Indeed, college climates characterized by a strong sense of direction tend to promote favorable outcomes (Davis and Murrell, 1993). "It is only by acting cooperatively in the context of common goals, as the most innovative institutions have done, that our accumulated understanding about student learning is put to best use" (Joint Task Force, 1998).

Keys to an Effective Merger

However, mergers of student affairs and academic affairs are only an opportunity for effective partnerships, not a guarantee of them. Indeed, without careful assessment and planning, such mergers can fail to have any positive effect on increasing collaboration or integrating the learning environment. In such cases, not only will the new structure fail to provide new opportunities for student affairs professionals to contribute to student learning, it may actually have a detrimental effect on student affairs professionals by isolating them from the president and other key decision makers within the institution. This isolation can diminish their ability to have a positive impact on students, even in traditional student affairs programs.

 'Once an institution has decided to merge students affairs within academic affairs in an attempt to develop more effective learning partnerships, the question becomes how to design the merger so it will be most effective. Obviously, just redrawing the organizational chart so student affairs is under the academic affairs "box" will not lead to any real enhancement of the campus learning environment; mergers of academic affairs and student affairs that are largely symbolic are unlikely to result in any real substantive change. For mergers to be effective they must transform how the institution views the learning environment; that is, it must see the learning environment as one coherent whole as opposed to a collection of separate pieces.

To accomplish this, student affairs staff, faculty, and academic administrators must be challenged to surrender traditional views of their roles. All should see themselves as engaged in a common enterprise, an enterprise in which the quality of learning is inseparable from the quality of community interactions and partnerships (Kellogg Commission, 1997). Student affairs staff, faculty, and academic administrators need to be involved in day-to-day learning opportunities: team-teaching, debating curriculum decisions, designing learning communities, assessing student outcomes. They will need to design structures that require learning across many disciplines, departments, and boundaries (Brown, 1997), thus requiring changes in attitudes, orientation, and responsibilities for every member of the academic community (Kellogg Commission, 1997). They will be confronted with new ideas, expectations, and demands that may fall outside their usual zones of comfort, and each must be ready to take risks and concede some "turf" for the venture to succeed.

For student affairs staff, it is necessary to overcome the "tyranny of custom" (Schroeder, 1996, p. 2) and leave the comfort, security, and predictability of traditional organizational boundaries to become learning-oriented professionals. Student affairs staff will be expected to develop programs that purposefully incorporate and identify learning contributions (Joint Task Force, 1998). They will need to shift their focus from administrative to educational concerns and construct a new understanding of how student affairs programs engender learning, acknowledging that programming and coordinating functions are not ends in themselves but vehicles by which to create learning and personal development opportunities (Cross, 1996; Kuh, 1996).

For faculty, the new learning environment will mean becoming involved not only in the classroom and lab but in all aspects of their institution's community life. They also, in turn, must expect and demand student participation in activities beyond the classroom. Academic administrators will need to make student learning and development an integral part of faculty and staff responsibilities and rewards, and all administrative leaders will need to rethink conventional organization to create more inventive structures and processes that integrate academic and student affairs (Joint Task Force, 1998).

For many faculty, staff, and administrators, this transformation of the learning environment means they will have to change not only what they do, but how they think (Kuh, 1996). In particular, they will have to reevaluate what they think about each other and their respective roles on campus. Cross (1996) stated that for the merger to succeed, turfs and specialties that have divided campuses for years will have to be replaced by faith and confidence in one's colleagues. Faculty, staff, and administrators must recognize that each person holds important knowledge and experience and has a role in student development and student learning. Moreover, a person's knowledge and experience may contribute outside their traditional role: "It is possible that the gifted faculty member could teach [student affairs professionals] a good deal about the whole student; and [student affairs professionals] could provide important perspective—beyond that which [they] now provide — on the classroom learning process and the life experience within which it is embodied" (Brown, 1997, p. 10).

Given historical differences in professional cultures, interaction among student affairs professionals, faculty, and academic administrators may not come easily. Therefore, the plan for merging student affairs and academic affairs must include intentional, relevant, and well-designed strategies to initiate and enhance the interaction that is vital to the institution's goals. Will student affairs staff be full members on key academic committees, or will they be appointed for the appearance of inclusiveness? Will research and sabbatical opportunities available to faculty also be available in some form to student affairs staff? Likewise, will faculty be meaningfully involved in workshops on student leadership development, staff training for student affairs, and out-of-class policy decisions? Will faculty be invited to conferences and professional development opportunities? If an institution cannot address these issues confidently, then it may not be ready to attempt a merger.

Political and Interpersonal Dynamics

In addition to historical differences in professional cultures, the effectiveness of an institution's merger of student affairs and academic affairs also may be affected significantly by the political and interpersonal dynamics that exist among institutional leaders. One factor to examine is the senior student affairs officer's organizational relationship to the institution's president and other administrative leaders on campus. In many mergers, the senior student affairs officer position will be included within academic affairs—usually as a dean of students (on some campuses it may be associate provost or similar title). This positioning can be beneficial for enhancing interaction with academic deans, faculty, and other key academic leaders; however, it also means that the senior student affairs officer may be one step further removed from the president, who often is the ultimate decision maker. To what extent this could affect merger effectiveness depends on the political and interpersonal dynamics that exist among campus leaders. The leaders most likely to influence the effectiveness of the merger are the provost (or academic vice president), academic deans and other academic administrators, the vice president for business affairs (or vice president for administration), and the president (or chancellor).

Provost. In many cases, the provost or academic vice president will be the leader who will oversee the new learning environment created by a merger; as a result, the provost will have enormous influence over the ultimate effectiveness of the merger. The provost does not need to be an expert on student affairs any more than he or she needs to be an expert on the humanities or health sciences; however, the provost should be an informed, interested advocate of the out-of-class learning environment just as he or she would be for the classroom environment. A provost who considers student affairs a collection of services rather than a valuable component of the learning environment, however, will not be able to provide the vision and leadership necessary to create a truly integrated learning environment.

Even if a provost values student affairs as an essential aspect of the learning environment, other characteristics of the provost can enhance or limit merger effectiveness. In day-to-day decision making, is the provost regularly mindful of student affairs or does it come as an afterthought to her or his other areas of responsibilities? Any progress will be slow if the provost is consistently reactive to out-of-class issues, responding to them only after they surface rather than making a concerted effort to integrate them into on-going academic plans.

However, the greatest impact the provost can have on the effectiveness of a merger of academic and student affairs is her or his influence on the interaction between student affairs staff—particularly the dean of students—and other academic leaders. Does the provost include the dean of students with the academic deans at their regular meetings? Is the dean of students invited to participate in deans' retreats, strategic planning sessions, or other important interaction opportunities? A dean of students who is removed from academic colleagues can be only a marginally effective partner in the campus learning environment.

Once the provost has included the dean of students as a member of the academic leadership team, it is critical that other team members consider the dean a legitimate partner on that team. Do the academic deans view the dean of students as a valuable asset to the learning environment, or do they see student affairs professionals as service staff whose primary value is to keep campus problems manageable? Even if the provost is an eager advocate of student affairs, the student affairs staff's ability to affect student learning will be limited if the other key academic leaders do not have ownership in the merger goals and objectives. Their ownership is essential to facilitating the meaningful faculty and student life interaction necessary for a truly integrated learning environment.

Vice President for Business Affairs. Although the staff most critical to an effective merger are inside academic affairs and student affairs, other campus leaders can have significant influence on the merger's effectiveness. One such person is the institution's senior financial officer, usually a vice president for business affairs or administration. This position is critical to the merger for two reasons. First, although the business affairs vice president may not be the ultimate decision maker in all financial matters, he or she usually has enormous influence over most financial decisions. Since many academic affairs–student affairs mergers require some financial investment or reallocation of resources, a vice president of business affairs who supports the merger's goals can serve as an important ally in identifying critical resources.

A second and similar reason the vice president for business affairs can affect merger effectiveness is her or his supervision of campus physical resources. As plans for an integrated learning environment develop, opportunities may arise to enhance the environment through the construction of new facilities or renovation of existing facilities; for example, creating classrooms or academic services in the residence halls may be seen as a pivotal step in the development of an integrated learning environment. Since the campus's physical plant and facilities often fall under the direction of the vice president for business affairs, he or she again is in a position to lend support to such ventures or raise objections to them. As in the case of academic leaders discussed above, the extent to which the vice president can be a contributor or barrier will be influenced by her or his ownership in the merger's goals and objectives.

The specific facilities and services managed by the vice president for business affairs also may influence the effectiveness of a student affairs–academic affairs merger. In particular, if the vice president supervises functions key to students' quality of life—such as residence halls, food services, and the student union—he or she has significantly greater influence on decisions critical to merger effectiveness. If the vice president for business affairs controls these functions but believes them to be vital components to student learning and quality of life, then he or she still can be a valuable ally in developing an integrated learning environment; however, if the vice president views these functions as auxiliary services whose primary role is to generate revenue, this support may be difficult to obtain.

President. Finally, as with most institutional ventures, the president's support is critical when attempting to merge student affairs within academic affairs. In some cases it may be the president who initiates such changes; in these instances, it is important for the president to communicate clearly how the academic affairs–student affairs merger fits into the larger vision for the institution.

However, in some cases the president may be a more removed player in the decision to merge these environments, viewing it simply as an organizational change rather than a fundamental shift in the development of the campus's learning environment; in this case, he or she may simply give consent when the idea is proposed by others. In instances when the president initiates the merger, merger leaders may be perceived as carrying out a presidential mandate, thus finding campus-wide support relatively easy to attain. However, when the president's support is not so obvious, the advocates of the merger may have to work harder to convert campus skeptics. As a result, these advocates may find it necessary to seek the president's support on individual issues as they arise.

In summary, an effective merger of academic affairs and student affairs is very difficult to accomplish by simply changing the organizational structure and seeing where it leads. Those designing an academic affairs–student affairs merger should first thoroughly develop goals for the learning environment. After the goals are in place, the merger designers should then assess the political and interpersonal dynamics that exist among the president, provost, dean of students, academic deans, vice president for business affairs, and other institutional leaders to gauge the level of support for the merger objectives. Once these steps are complete, the institution will be in a position to determine the potential for an effective, integrated learning environment.

Important Questions to Address Before Merging

Institutional leaders considering merging academic affairs and student affairs should consider the following questions before making a final decision:

1. Is the merger initiated by the possibility for budget savings or an enhanced, integrated learning environment?
2. Is the provost committed to initiating interaction among student affairs staff, academic deans, and other academic staff? Or is he or she willing to invest appropriate energy and resources in a plan developed by others?
3. Will the provost be an informed, active advocate of out-of-class learning to the president and other institutional leaders?
4. Are student affairs professionals, faculty, and academic administrators willing to abandon their traditional roles and take risks that might cause discomfort?
5. Are key quality-of-life functions (housing, food service, student union, and so forth) under the supervision of business affairs?
6. Does the business vice president value student affairs and out-of-class learning? Is there a positive, healthy relationship between student affairs staff and business affairs staff? (This becomes increasingly important if business affairs supervises key quality-of-life areas.)
7. Does the president have experience with or value for student affairs and out-of-class learning? Is the president willing to support out-of-class learning as integral to the institution's larger learning goals?

The character of the responses to these questions might or might not preclude a merger but at the very least should alert institutional leaders to potential problems. Examples of successful mergers include Roger Ballou's description of efforts at the University of Wisconsin-River Falls (Ballou, 1997).

Implications for Student Affairs Professionals

The merging of academic affairs and student affairs has significant implications—potentially positive or negative—on the institution's learning environment and its students. Likewise, an academic affairs–student affairs merger also may have implications for the student affairs professionals who work in it. If the merger is effective, the professional will have opportunities to develop valuable skills and experience in some new areas, such as curriculum, teaching, learning communities, research, and outcomes assessment. In addition to these tangible skills benefits, student affairs professionals may experience higher job satisfaction when recognized as a valuable part of the institution's core learning environment.

If the merger is not well designed, however, and the new structure fails to provide a meaningful role for student affairs staff in the learning environment, the staff may feel isolated from the institution's learning environment as well as key institutional decision makers. As a result, student affairs staff may feel they have limited influence on decisions affecting quality-of-life issues—let alone institutional learning goals—which can discourage their efforts to work at collaboration with others outside their department or area.

Conclusion

Institutions desiring to develop meaningful partnerships among faculty, academic administrators, and student affairs professionals may find they can facilitate this through merging student affairs within the division of academic affairs. This structure has the potential to encourage greater interaction and become a catalyst for developing exciting learning partnerships on campus. Mergers grounded in the shared desire to make the student affairs mission and the academic affairs mission integrated components of one comprehensive, institutional learning environment are the most likely to result in a positive impact on the learning environment. To make the merger work, faculty, academic administrators, and student affairs professionals may need to overcome boundaries inherent in their traditional campus roles; it also is important to consider how the political and interpersonal dynamics that exist among institutional leaders may affect merger effectiveness. Finally, student affairs professionals need to be particularly mindful of the implications—both positive and negative—a student affairs–academic affairs merger may have on their work and their career.

References

Ballou, R. A. "Reorganizing Student Affairs for the Twenty-First Century." *About Campus,* 1997, 2 (5), 24–25.

Brown, J. S. "On Becoming a Learning Organization." *About Campus,* 1997, 1 (6), 5–13.

Cross, K. P. "New Lenses on Learning." *About Campus,* 1996, 1 (1), 4–9.

Davis, T. M., and Murrell, P. H. *Turning Teaching Into Learning: The Role of Student Responsibility in the Collegiate Experience.* Washington, D.C.: The George Washington University, School of Education and Human Development, 1993. (ASHE-ERIC Higher Education Report No. 8.)

Joint Task Force on Student Learning. *Powerful Partnerships: A Shared Responsibility for Learning.* Washington, D.C.: National Association of Student Personnel Administrators, 1998.

Kellogg Commission on the Future of State and Land Grant Universities. *Returning to Our Roots: The Student Experience.* Washington, D.C.: National Association of State Universities and Land Grant Colleges, 1997.

Kuh, G. D. "Some Things We Should Forget." *About Campus,* 1996, 1 (4), 10–15.

Schroeder, C. C. "Enhancing Undergraduate Education: An Imperative for Student Affairs." *About Campus,* 1996, 1 (4), 2–3.

JERRY PRICE is dean of students at Drake University in Des Moines, Iowa.

Evaluating the impact of partnerships on the campus climate and culture is an important step in developing partnerships between academic and student affairs.

Guiding Principles for Evaluating Student and Academic Affairs Partnerships

John H. Schuh

Once partnerships have been formed between academic and student affairs, mechanisms need to be put in place to evaluate the extent to which these partnerships have been successful. Although other partnerships may be developed to improve institutional functioning and efficiency, or for other reasons, student learning would be the primary purpose of academic and student affairs partnerships. Garland and Grace (1993, citing Seldin and Associates, 1990), describe the situation this way: The failure of colleges to establish links between students' out-of-classroom experiences and their academic endeavors has impeded not only students' overall personal development but also the quality of their academic experience. Terenzini (1993) adds that if academic and student affairs units work together, students are likely to benefit from such collaboration. Looking to the future, Murphy (1989) recommends that "the distance that exists between student and academic affairs should best be viewed as past history" (p. 377).

Previous chapters in this sourcebook have described various methods of evaluating the outcomes of partnerships between academic and student affairs. It is clear that a wide variety of approaches is available to academic and student affairs administrators who wish to evaluate the success of their joint activities. Space limitations preclude the authors from providing detailed descriptions of techniques and approaches to evaluation and assessment, but useful sources of such information include Banta and Associates, 1993; Banta, Lund, Black, and Oblander, 1996; Blimling, Whitt, and Associates, 1999; Kuh, 1993; Kuh, Schuh, Whitt, and Associates, 1991; Stage, 1992; and Upcraft and Schuh, 1996.

This chapter shifts our focus on evaluation from student outcomes to the general impact academic and student affairs partnerships have on the climate and culture of the institutions in which they occur. A series of principles that illustrate successful partnerships is provided. The list can be used to do a quick check of the landscape of your institution. The more evidence of these principles on a given campus, the greater the likelihood that effective partnerships have been formed between academic and student affairs. Of course the extent to which these principles are perceived as permeating the fabric of a campus is a matter of judgment, and two individuals on the same campus might view the same situation in substantially different ways. Even if that is the case, these principles can be used to stimulate discussion about partnerships: To what extent do they exist on your campus and how do they influence the institution? Which partnerships are most effective and why? How are effective partnerships formed? What obstacles exist to forming effective partnerships? How can they improve institutional effectiveness? How can existing partnerships be enhanced?

Clearly the list of principles is incomplete. In specific situations, other items could be added to the list, or some could be deleted from it. The way that institutions develop partnerships depends very much on their students and their circumstances (Chickering and Gamson, 1987; Schroeder, 1999). But the important point is that conversations need to occur about partnerships on the individual campus, before they are formed, while they are in the process of being developed, and after the fact as well.

Principles that Demonstrate Effective Partnerships

1. Student learning is an essential part of the institution's mission. All members of the institution are deeply committed to student learning and use that commitment to guide their work. And the commitment to learning is manifested in the life of the campus: "Both mission statements and goals must be used to be useful, and evidence suggests in all too many cases we are not using them (Gardiner, 1994, p. 108).

Lyons (1993) points out that institutional mission shapes student affairs work. The consequence of this observation for student learning is clear: "The greater priority that the faculty or administration assign to student learning and development as an institution goal, the greater the respect and support accorded to student affairs" (Astin, 1996, p. 132).

2. Student learning is the organizing principle of the student experience. What this principle means is that as programs are considered for addition or deletion, the first question asked is, "How will this change affect student learning?" Although financial or organizational reasons will not be discounted entirely, student learning will be the focus of the institution's leaders. Kuh, Douglas, Lund, and Ramin-Gyurnek (1994) point out that "Institutions with an ethos of learning are blessed with more than a few boundary spanners, peo-

ple who move among the functional silos, articulating the institution's mission and vision with language that acknowledges and respects both classroom and out-of-class learning" (p. 64).

Institutional messages to prospective students emphasize the importance of student learning, whether by the institution's view book, catalog, or other information to new students. Orientation activities emphasize the importance of student learning, and student learning will be evaluated continuously throughout their experiences. Faculty members use a learning-centered approach to instruction. A wide variety of instructional technologies is employed in the classroom, but the traditional lecture is used sparingly. Students' out-of-class learning experiences are recognized and rewarded. Through convocations, institutional ceremonies, scholarship awards, and other institutional activities, student learning is celebrated.

3. The learning process for students is seamless. "The word *seamless* suggests that what was once believed to be separate, distinct parts (e.g., in-class and out-of-class, academic and nonacademic, curricular and cocurricular, or on-campus and off-campus experiences) are now of one piece, bound together so as to appear whole or continuous" (Kuh, 1996, p. 136). This suggests that student learning should occur in virtually all corners of the campus at all times. Indeed, learning occurs in the classroom, on the intramural field, in the residence hall, the library, sites of student work, and other places on the campus. "The intellectual, social, and emotional elements of learning can be integrated in and out of the classroom" (Love and Love, 1995, p. 78). The institution recognizes that student learning could occur anywhere on campus, and in other, purposeful, experiences that would occur off campus, such as volunteer activities, student work and so on.

4. Credit experiences require out-of-class activities. This evaluation criterion means that the application of learning experiences occurs outside the classroom. In practical terms this means that internships and cooperative education experiences are highly valued, as they should be, because there is strong evidence to suggest that such experiences are powerful sources of desired learning outcomes (Astin and Sax, 1998). It also means that service learning is an essential element in the curriculum so that students must complete certain activities outside of the classroom before earning credit. To be sure, not all disciplines lend themselves to such experiences, but as out-of-class learning experiences complement the nature of the curriculum, these experiences should be integrated into student learning experiences. Faculty consider integrating out-of-class learning experiences into the curriculum a priority rather than as an afterthought. "Courses employing service-learning encourage students to ask the larger questions of life beyond the bounds of most traditional courses. Not only does service-learning have the potential to help students learn the content in a particular discipline, it also asks students to consider the context of a discipline and how its knowledge base is used in practice" (Enos and Troppe, 1996, p. 156).

5. Student affairs staff coteach courses with faculty. Suggesting that student affairs practitioners can coteach any course is patently ludicrous, but a substantial number of courses can be offered by student affairs officers with faculty. Heading the list are first-year seminars for entering students. Upcraft, Gardner, and Associates (1989) indicate that faculty, administrators, or professional staff can teach such courses. Much of the content of these courses is mastered by student affairs staff who have been offering workshops and other learning experiences for students on time management, stress reduction, and organizational skills for years. These seminars provide a natural match for student affairs practitioners and faculty.

A second area where collaboration in offering courses has great potential is diversity education. Astin (1996) pointed out that diversity education has a positive effect on students. This form of activity is a sure-fire winner for everyone involved—for students in terms of their learning, for faculty who will form a valuable partnership with student affairs practitioners in developing curriculum, and for student affairs staff in playing an increasingly central role in the life of the university. Other areas of course content where partnerships are possible include leadership development, an important outcome of the higher education experience, and career planning and development.

In some situations, campus alliances (see Sagaria and Johnsrud, 1989) can be developed and student affairs staff can coordinate an entire program, such as a freshman year experience. Similar approaches are being taken toward other initiatives, such as the establishment of learning communities.

Finally, student affairs practitioners consult routinely with faculty in the delivery of instruction. As is mentioned above, certain forms of learning are more effective than others (for example, see Love and Love, 1995, p. 48), and student affairs practitioners commonly are familiar with these forms of learning. In an institution where partnerships are formed easily and effectively, student affairs practitioners work regularly with faculty in sharing their ideas about the delivery of instruction.

6. Students describe learning as continuous. One of the best ways to learn about how students learn is to ask them (Kuh, 1993). Students are very perceptive and refreshing in describing their experiences. In a college where student and academic affairs partnerships are formed easily and effectively, one consequence is that students describe their learning experiences as occurring at all times and in all places. "Effective learning environments elicit the convergence of all the student's learning experiences" (Schroeder and Hurst, 1996, p. 175). For example, students report that they have been immersed in a rich learning environment during the course of their college career. Cross (1996, p. 9) raises an interesting question: "I wonder what responses would be forthcoming if at the conclusion of a spirited student council debate, council members were asked to write about what they had learned about themselves, about cooperation, or about leadership from the meeting?" They may not be able to pinpoint exactly where or how they developed a certain skill, but they will report that what occurred in and out of the classroom was complementary.

They will also report that faculty members recognize and affirm the value of the learning that occurs outside the classroom.

7. Faculty interact regularly with students outside the classroom. "Student-faculty contact and student learning are positively related, and it would seem that finding ways to promote such contact is in the best educational interests of both students and institutions" (Terenzini, Pascarella, and Blimling, 1996, p. 155). This means that faculty serve as fellows in the residence halls, advise student organizations, attend student events, and by their presence affirm the value of the out-of-class experience. Clearly, this principle has implications for the promotion and tenure process. Faculty time is precious, and every hour spent interacting with students outside the classroom is one less hour that faculty have for research and creative activity. Also, not all faculty members are adept at informal interaction with students. They do not all enjoy playing volleyball, attending tailgate parties, advising departmental clubs, or other forms of informal interaction with students. Other faculty have such robust research agendas that they simply do not have time for these activities. But there are many faculty members, especially those who have successfully negotiated the promotion and tenure process, who may be available and would enjoy this kind of activity. One way of determining the extent to which academic and student affairs partnerships are successfully formed would be to evaluate how frequently and in what context faculty interact with students outside the classroom.

8. Institutional committees and task forces include balanced representation of faculty and student affairs practitioners. This principle cuts both ways in that, historically, student affairs officers have expressed concern about being full institutional partners with faculty members. Student affairs practitioners have expressed concern about being junior partners in the institution's decision-making process but have overlooked that faculty often are left out of the decision-making process in other areas of the institution. For example, whereas student affairs officers might not sit on bodies that make decisions about curriculum, faculty might not sit on committees related to financial aid, the operation of the residence halls, or the apportioning of student fees. No element of an institution's family (faculty, staff, students, or graduates) is any more informed, insightful, or prescient than any other regarding aspects outside its purview. Faculty are not expert in operating residence halls, and student affairs staff possess no special gifts in determining requirements for earning a degree. But representation from all elements of an institution can contribute to the strength of the decision-making process. Garland and Grace (1993) assert that when faculty and student affairs staff work together, good things happen. "Working together, faculty and student affairs professionals can combine talents to better serve students and the institution" (p. 62). Simple questions such as, "Why do we do things this way" or "How does that philosophy fit with our college's mission?" require those responsible for the particular area to examine why they have taken the approach they have.

9. The development of learning communities is widely supported on campus. Learning communities have been demonstrated to contribute to the potency of the student experience. A body of research exists that clearly underscores the value of such experiences for students (see Light, 1992; Astin, 1996; Cross, 1998). But student affairs staff and faculty need to work together. Kuh (1996) asserts that "all members of an institution must work together to link programs across the academic and out-of-class dimensions of students' lives" (p. 137). These communities require the appropriation of resources—faculty time, administrative support, and perhaps financial resources—to make them occur. In a campus where collaboration is common and it is easy to form partnerships, support for this activity is widespread. That does not mean that a blank check would be available to support anything faculty or student affairs staff would want to do, but that support for improving the student learning experience is a part of the institutional culture.

A Final Word

The principles introduced in this chapter provide some ideas that can be used to evaluate the effectiveness of partnerships formed by academic and student affairs. Other sources exist that describe partnerships in great detail (for example, the American Association for Higher Education, American College Personnel Association, and National Association of Student Personnel Administrators [AAHE, ACPA, NASPA] Joint Task Force report *Powerful Partnerships*, 1998). No doubt there are other concepts that can be applied to specific situations. We think this is good place to start the conversation about the evaluation process. Other steps can be taken to do a thorough job of evaluating these partnerships.

References

American Association for Higher Education, American College Personnel Association, and National Association of Student Personnel Administrators (Joint Task Force). *Powerful Partnerships: A Shared Responsibility for Learning.* [http://www.naspa.org]. June 1998.

Astin, A. W. "Involvement in Learning Revisited: Lessons We Have Learned." *Journal of College Student Development,* 1996, *37* (2),123–134.

Astin, A. W., and Sax, L. J. "How Undergraduates Are Affected by Service Participation." *Journal of College Student Development,* 1998, *39* (3), 251–263.

Banta, T. W., and others. *Making a Difference: Outcomes of a Decade of Assessment in Higher Education.* San Francisco: Jossey-Bass, 1993.

Banta, T. W., Lund, J. P., Black, K. E., and Oblander, F. W. *Assessment in Practice: Putting Principles to Work on College Campuses.* San Francisco: Jossey-Bass, 1996.

Blimling, G. S., Whitt, E. J., and others. *Good Practice in Student Affairs: Principles to Foster Student Learning.* San Francisco: Jossey-Bass, 1999.

Chickering, A. W., and Gamson, Z. F. "Seven Principles for Good Practice in Undergraduate Education." *AAHE Bulletin,* 1987, *39* (7), 3–7.

Cross, K. P. "New Lenses on Learning." *About Campus,* 1996, *1,* (1), 4–9.

Cross, K. P. "Why Learning Communities? Why Now?" *About Campus,* 1998, *3* (3), 4–11.

Gardiner, L. F. *Redesigning Higher Education: Producing Dramatic Gains in Student Learning.* Washington, D.C.: The George Washington University, School of Education and Human Development, 1994. (ASHE-ERIC Higher Education Report no. 7.)

Garland, P. H., and Grace, T. W. *New Perspectives for Student Affairs Professionals: Evolving Realities, Responsibilities, and Roles.* Washington, D.C.: The George Washington University, School of Education and Human Development, 1993. (ASHE-ERIC Higher Education Report no. 7.)

Enos, S. L., and Troppe, M. L. "Service-Learning in the Curriculum." In B. Jacoby and others, *Service-Learning in Higher Education.* San Francisco: Jossey-Bass, 1996, 156–181.

Kuh, G. D. "In Their Own Words: What Students Learn Outside the Classroom." *American Educational Research Journal,* 1993, *30* (20), 277–304.

Kuh, G. D. "Guiding Principles for Creating Seamless Learning Environment for Undergraduates." *Journal of College Student Development,* 1996, *37* (2), 135–148.

Kuh, G. D., Douglas, K. B., Lund, J. P., and Ramin-Gyurnek, J. *Student Learning Outside the Classroom: Transcending Artificial Boundaries.* Washington, D.C.: The George Washington University, School of Education and Human Development, 1994. (ASHE-ERIC Higher Education Report no. 8.)

Kuh, G. D., Schuh, J. H., Whitt, E. J., and Associates. *Involving Colleges: Successful Approaches to Fostering Student Learning and Development Outside the Classroom.* San Francisco: Jossey-Bass, 1991.

Light, R. J. *The Harvard Assessment Seminars. Second Report: Explorations with Students and Faculty about Teaching, Learning, and Student Life.* Cambridge, Mass.: Harvard University, 1992.

Love, P. G., and Love, A. G. *Enhancing Student Learning: Intellectual, Social, and Emotional Integration.* Washington, D.C.: The George Washington University, School of Education and Human Development, 1995. (ASHE-ERIC Higher Education Report no. 4.)

Lyons, J. W. "The Importance of Institutional Mission." In M. J. Barr and Associates (eds.), *The Handbook of Student Affairs Administration.* San Francisco: Jossey-Bass, 1993.

Murphy, R. O. "Academic and Student Affairs in Partnership for Freshman Success." In M. L. Upcraft, J. N. Gardner, and others (eds.), *The Freshman Year Experience.* San Francisco: Jossey-Bass, 1989.

Sagaria, M.A.D., and Johnsrud, L. K. "Providing Administrative, Faculty, and Staff Leadership." In M. L. Upcraft, J. N. Gardner, and others (eds.), *The Freshman Year Experience.* San Francisco: Jossey-Bass, 1989.

Schroeder, C. C. "Forging Educational Partnerships to Advance Student Learning" In G. S. Blimling and E. J. Whitt (eds.), *Good Practice in Student Affairs: Principles to Foster Student Learning.* San Francisco: Jossey-Bass, 1999.

Schroeder, C. C., and Hurst, J. C. "Designing Learning Environments that Integrate Curricular and Cocurricular Experiences." *Journal of College Student Development,* 1996, *37* (2), 174–181.

Stage, F. K. "The Case for Flexibility in Research and Assessment of College Students." In F. K. Stage (ed.), *Diverse Methods for Research and Assessment of College Students.* Alexandria, Va.: American College Personnel Association, 1992, 1–12.

Terenzini, P. T. *Influences Affecting the Development of Students' Critical Thinking Skills.* University Park, Penna.: National Center on Postsecondary Teaching, Learning, and Assessment, 1993. (ERIC Document no. ED 372666.)

Terenzini, P. T., Pascarella, E. T., and Blimling, G. S. "Students' Out-of-Class Experiences and Their Influence on Learning and Cognitive Development: A Literature Review." *Journal of College Student Development,* 1996, *37* (2), 149–162.

Upcraft, M. L., Gardner, J. N., and others. *The Freshman Year Experience: Helping Students Survive and Succeed in College.* San Francisco: Jossey-Bass, 1989.

Upcraft, M. L., and Schuh, J. H. (eds.). *Assessment in Student Affairs.* San Francisco: Jossey-Bass, 1996.

JOHN H. SCHUH is professor of educational leadership and policy studies at Iowa State University.

INDEX

93

Back Issue/Subscription Order Form

Copy or detach and send to:
Jossey-Bass Inc., Publishers, 350 Sansome Street, San Francisco CA 94104-1342

Call or fax toll free!
Phone 888-378-2537 6AM–5PM PST; Fax 800-605-2665

Back issues: Please send me the following issues at $23 each.

(Important: please include series initials and issue number, such as SS90.)

1. SS _____

_____

_____

$ _____ Total for single issues

$ _____ Shipping charges (for single issues *only;* subscriptions are exempt
from shipping charges): Up to $30, add $5^{50} • $30^{01}–$50, add $6^{50}
$50^{01}–$75, add $7^{50} • $75^{01}–$100, add $9 • $100^{01}–$150, add $10
Over $150, call for shipping charge.

Subscriptions   Please ❑ start   ❑ renew my subscription to *New Directions
for Student Services* for the year _____ at the following rate:

❑ Individual $58   ❑ Institutional $104

NOTE: Subscriptions are quarterly and are for the calendar year only.
Subscriptions begin with the spring issue of the year indicated above.
For shipping outside the U.S., please add $25.

$ _____ Total single issues and subscriptions (CA, IN, NJ, NY, and DC
residents, add sales tax for single issues. NY and DC residents must
include shipping charges when calculating sales tax. NY and Canadian
residents only, add sales tax for subscriptions.)

❑ Payment enclosed (U.S. check or money order only)
❑ VISA, MC, AmEx, Discover Card #_____ Exp. date_____

Signature _____ Day phone _____
❑ Bill me (U.S. institutional orders only. Purchase order required.)

Purchase order #_____

Name _____

Address _____

_____

Phone_____ E-mail _____

For more information about Jossey-Bass Publishers, visit our Web site at:
www.josseybass.com   **PRIORITY CODE = ND1**